JUMP Math 6.1

Book 6 Part 1 of 2

Contents

jump math™

MULTIPLYING POTENTIAL.

JUMP Math
Toronto, Ontario
www.jumpmath.org

Writers: Dr. John Mighton, Dr. Sindi Sabourin, Dr. Anna Klebanov
Consultant: Jennifer Wyatt
Cover Design: Blakeley Words+Pictures
Special thanks to the design and layout team.
Cover Photograph: © iStockphoto.com/Grafissimo

ISBN: 978-1-897120-77-4

Sixth printing June 2013

Preserving our environment

Jump Math chose to print the pages of this book on recycled paper and saved these resources[1]:

energy	water	greenhouse gases	solid waste
326 million BTUs	1,294,778 L	33,172 kg	10,754 kg

Printed by **Webcom Inc.** on Legacy Brite 100%

ANCIENT FOREST™ FRIENDLY

770 trees were saved for our forests

RECYCLED **100%** RECYCLABLE
Legacy Brite 100%
Printed by **Webcom Inc.**

[1]Estimates were made using the Environmental Defense Paper Calculator.

This book was manufactured without the use of additional coatings or processes, and was assembled using the latest equipment to achieve almost zero waste. Manufacturing this book in Canada ensures compliance with strict environmental practices and eliminates the need for international freight, which is a major contributor to global air pollution.

Printed and bound in Canada

A note to educators, parents, and everyone who believes that numeracy is as important as literacy for a fully functioning society

Welcome to JUMP Math

Entering the world of JUMP Math means believing that every child has the capacity to be fully numerate and to love math. Founder and mathematician John Mighton has used this premise to develop his innovative teaching method. The resulting materials isolate and describe concepts so clearly and incrementally that everyone can understand them.

JUMP Math is comprised of workbooks, teacher's guides, evaluation materials, outreach programs, tutoring support through schools and community organizations, and provincial curriculum correlations. All of this is presented on the JUMP Math website: **www.jumpmath.org**.

Teacher's guides are available on the website for free use. Read the introduction to the teacher's guides before you begin using these materials. This will ensure that you understand both the philosophy and the methodology of JUMP Math. The workbooks are designed for use by children, with adult guidance. Each child will have unique needs and it is important to provide the child with the appropriate support and encouragement as he or she works through the material.

Allow children to discover the concepts on the worksheets by themselves as much as possible. Mathematical discoveries can be made in small, incremental steps. The discovery of a new step is like untangling the parts of a puzzle. It is exciting and rewarding.

Children will need to answer the questions marked with a in a notebook. Grid paper and notebooks should always be on hand for answering extra questions or when additional room for calculation is needed. Grid paper is also available in the BLM section of the Teacher's Guide.

The means "Stop! Assess understanding and explain new concepts before proceeding."

Contents

PART 1
Patterns & Algebra

Number Sense

Measurement

Probability & Data Management

Geometry

PART 2
Patterns & Algebra

Number Sense

Measurement

Probability & Data Management

Geometry

PA6-1: Increasing Sequences

In an **increasing sequence**, each number is greater than the one before it.

Deborah wants to continue the number pattern:

6 , 8 , 10 , 12 , _?_

She finds the **difference**
between the first two numbers:

6   7   8

②
6 , 8 , 10 , 12 , _?_

She finds that the difference between the other numbers in
the pattern is also 2. So the pattern was made by adding 2:

② ② ②
6 , 8 , 10 , 12 , _?_

To continue the pattern, Deborah adds 2 to the last number
in the sequence.

The final number in the pattern is 14:

② ② ② ②
6 , 8 , 10 , 12 , 14

----

1. Extend the following patterns. Start by finding the gap between the numbers.

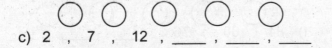

a) 2 , 5 , 8 , ____ , ____ , ____   b) 1 , 7 , 13 , ____ , ____ , ____

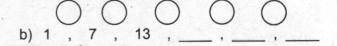

c) 2 , 7 , 12 , ____ , ____ , ____   d) 4 , 8 , 12 , ____ , ____ , ____

e) 1 , 6 , 11 , ____ , ____ , ____   f) 4 , 10 , 16 , ____ , ____ , ____

g) 2 , 12 , 22 , ____ , ____ , ____   h) 7 , 15 , 23 , ____ , ____ , ____

i) 31 , 34 , 37 , ____ , ____ , ____   j) 92 , 98 , 104 , ____ , ____ , ____

k) 12 , 23 , 34 , ____ , ____ , ____   l) 0 , 8 , 16 , ____ , ____ , ____

2. A plant that is 17 cm high grows 2 cm each day.

a) How high will the plant be after three days? _____

b) In how many days will the plant be 27 cm high? _____

In a **decreasing sequence**, each number is less than the one before it.

Inder wants to continue the number pattern:

25 , 23 , 21 , _?_

She finds the **difference**
between the first two numbers:

25   24   23

$\overbrace{25}^{-2}$, 23 , 21 , _?_

She finds that the difference between the other numbers in the pattern
is also 2. So the pattern was made by subtracting 2.

25 , 23 , 21 , ? (-2)(-2)

The final number in the pattern is 19:

25 , 23 , 21 , 19 (-2)(-2)(-2)

- -

1. Extend the following patterns:

   a) 18 , 15 , 12 , ___ , ___ , ___

   b) 32 , 26 , 20 , ___ , ___ , ___

   c) 52 , 47 , 42 , ___ , ___ , ___

   d) 34 , 30 , 26 , ___ , ___ , ___

   e) 51 , 46 , 41 , ___ , ___ , ___

   f) 84 , 80 , 76 , ___ , ___ , ___

   g) 62 , 51 , 40 , ___ , ___ , ___

   h) 97 , 89 , 81 , ___ , ___ , ___

   i) 71 , 64 , 57 , ___ , ___ , ___

   j) 62 , 58 , 54 , ___ , ___ , ___

   k) 82 , 73 , 64 , ___ , ___ , ___

   l) 84 , 72 , 60 , ___ , ___ , ___

Use decreasing sequences to solve these problems:

2. Judi has saved $49. She spends $8 each day.
   How much money does she have left after 5 days?

3. Yen has a roll of 74 stamps. She uses 7 each day for 4 days.
   How many are left?

48¢

PA6-3: Extending a Pattern Using a Rule

1. Continue the following sequences by <u>adding</u> the number given:

   a) (add 4)   41, 45, _____, _____, _____

   b) (add 8)   60, 68, _____, _____, _____

   c) (add 3)   74, 77, _____, _____, _____

   d) (add 11)   20, 31, _____, _____, _____

   e) (add 8)   61, 69, _____, _____, _____

   f) (add 11)   31, 42, _____, _____, _____

2. Continue the following sequences, <u>subtracting</u> by the number given:

   a) (subtract 3)   25, 22, _____, _____, _____

   b) (subtract 2)   34, 32, _____, _____, _____

   c) (subtract 6)   85, 79, _____, _____, _____

   d) (subtract 12)   89, 77, _____, _____, _____

   e) (subtract 8)   57, 49, _____, _____, _____

   f) (subtract 7)   57, 50, _____, _____, _____

BONUS

3. Create a pattern of your own. After writing the pattern in the blanks, say what you added or subtracted each time:

   _____ , _____ , _____ , _____ , _____   My rule: _____

4. Which one of the following sequences was made by adding 7? Circle it:
   HINT: Check all the numbers in the sequence.

   a) 4, 10, 18, 21   b) 4, 11, 16, 21   c) 3, 10, 17, 24

5.   **72, 61, 50, 39, 28 ...**

   Brenda says this sequence was made by subtracting 12 each time.

   Sanjukta says it was made by subtracting 11.

   Who is right?

   _____

   _____

PA6-4: Identifying Pattern Rules

1. What number was added to make the sequence?

    a) 12, 17, 22, 27   add ____   b) 32, 35, 38, 41   add ____

    c) 28, 34, 40, 46   add ____   d) 50, 57, 64, 71   add ____

    e) 101, 106, 111, 116   add ____   f) 269, 272, 275, 278   add ____

2. What number was subtracted to make the sequence?

    a) 58, 56, 54, 52   subtract ____   b) 75, 70, 65, 60   subtract ____

    c) 320, 319, 318, 317   subtract ____   d) 191, 188, 185, 182   subtract ____

    e) 467, 461, 455, 449   subtract ____   f) 939, 937, 935, 933   subtract ____

3. State the rules for the following patterns:

    a) 419, 412, 405, 398, 391   subtract ____   b) 311, 319, 327, 335, 343, 351   add ____

    c) 501, 505, 509, 513   _____   d) 210, 199, 188, 177,   _____

    e) 653, 642, 631, 620, 609   _____   f) 721, 730, 739, 748, 757, 766   _____

    g) 807, 815, 823, 831   _____   h) 1731, 1725, 1719, 1713,   _____

4. Use the first three numbers in the pattern to find the rule. Then fill in the blanks:

    a) 52, 57, 62, __67__, _____, _____   The rule is: ___Start at 52 and add 5_____

    b) 78, 75, 72, _____, _____, _____   The rule is: _____

    c) 824, 836, 848, _____, _____, _____   The rule is: _____

    d) 1 328, 1 319, 1 310, _____, _____, _____   The rule is: _____

5.   **5, 11, 17, 23, 29 ...**

    Tim says the pattern rule is: "Start at 5 and subtract 6 each time."

    Jack says the rule is: "Add 5 each time."

    Hannah says the rule is: "Start at 5 and add 6 each time."

    a) Whose rule is correct? _____

    b) What mistakes did the others make? _____

    _____

jump math
MULTIPLYING POTENTIAL.

Claude creates an **increasing pattern** with squares. He records the number of squares in each figure in a chart or T-table. He also records the number of squares he adds each time he makes a new figure:

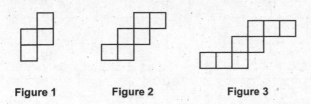

| Figure 1 | Figure 2 | Figure 3 |

Figure	# of Squares
1	4
2	6
3	8

2
2

Number of squares added each time

The number of squares in the figures are 4, 6, 8, …

Claude writes a rule for this number pattern:

RULE: Start at 4 and add 2 each time.

- -

1. Claude makes other <u>increasing patterns</u> with squares.

    How many squares does he add to make each new figure?

    Write your answer in the circles provided. Then write a rule for the pattern:

a)

Figure	Number of Squares
1	2
2	8
3	14

Rule:

b)

Figure	Number of Squares
1	3
2	9
3	15

Rule:

c)

Figure	Number of Squares
1	1
2	6
3	11

Rule:

d)

Figure	Number of Squares
1	1
2	8
3	15

Rule:

e)

Figure	Number of Squares
1	5
2	13
3	21

Rule:

f)

Figure	Number of Squares
1	11
2	22
3	33

Rule:

g)

Figure	Number of Squares
1	3
2	12
3	21

Rule:

h)

Figure	Number of Squares
1	6
2	13
3	20

Rule:

i)

Figure	Number of Squares
1	7
2	13
3	19

Rule:

2. Extend the number pattern. How many squares would be used in Figure 6?

a)

Figure	Number of Squares
1	2
2	10
3	18

b)

Figure	Number of Squares
1	4
2	9
3	14

c)

Figure	Number of Squares
1	7
2	11
3	15

3. After making Figure 3, Claude only has 35 squares left. Does he have enough squares to complete Figure 4?

a)

Figure	Number of Squares
1	4
2	13
3	22

YES   NO

b)

Figure	Number of Squares
1	6
2	17
3	28

YES   NO

c)

Figure	Number of Squares
1	9
2	17
3	25

YES   NO

4. In your notebook, make a T-table to show how many shapes will be needed to make the fifth figure in each pattern:

a)

b)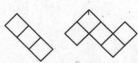

1. Count the number of line segments (lines that join pairs of dots) in each set of figures by marking each line segment as you count, as shown in the example:

   HINT: Count around the outside of the figure first.

   Example:

   a) 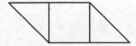 _____   b) 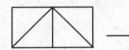 _____   c) _____

2. Continue the pattern below, then complete the chart:

   Figure 1

   Figure 2

   Figure 3

   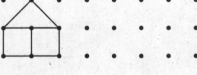
   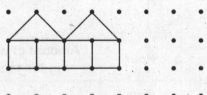

Figure	Number of Line Segments
1	
2	
3	

   a) How many line segments would Figure 4 have? _____

   b) How many line segments would you need to make a figure with 5 triangles? _____

3. Continue the pattern below, then complete the chart:

   Figure 1

   Figure 2

   Figure 3

   Figure 4

   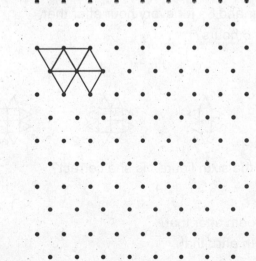

Figure	Number of Triangles	Number of Line Segments

   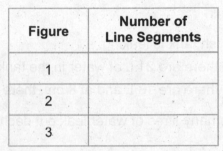

   a) How many line segments would Figure 5 have? _____

   b) How many triangles would Figure 6 have?

   _____

4. The snow is 17 cm deep at 5 pm.
    4 cm of snow falls each hour.
    How deep is the snow at 9 pm?

Hour	Depth of Snow
5 pm	17 cm

5. Philip has $42 in savings by the end of July.
    Each month he saves $9. How much will he have by the end of October?

Month	Savings
July	$42

6. Sarah's fish tank is leaking.
    At 6 pm, there are 21 L of water in the tank.
    At 7 pm, there are 18 L and at 8 pm, there are 15 L.

    a) How many litres of water leak out each hour?

    _____

    b) How many litres will be left in the tank at 10 pm?

    _____

    c) How many hours will it take for all the water
        to leak out?

    _____

Hour	Amount of water in the tank
6 pm	21 L
7 pm	18 L
8 pm	15 L
9 pm	
10 pm	

7. A store rents snowboards at $7 for the first hour and $5 for every hour after that.
    How much does it cost to rent a snowboard for 6 hours?

8. a) How many triangles would April need to make
        a figure with 10 squares?

 1   2   3

    b) April says that she needs 15 triangles to make the sixth figure. Is she correct?

9. Merle saves $55 in August. She saves $6 each month after that.
    Alex saves $42 in August. He saves $7 each month after that.
    Who has saved the most money by the end of January?

PA6-7: T-tables (Advanced)

The **terms** of a sequence are the numbers or items in the sequence.

A **term number** gives the position of each item.

This is **term number 4** since it is in the fourth position.

$$4, \ 7, \ 10, \ 13, \ 16$$

----

1. Draw a T-table for each sequence to find the given term:

    a) Find the 5th term: 3, 8, 13, 18, …   b) Find the 7th term: 42, 46, 50, 54,…

2. Ben says that the 6th term of the sequence 7, 13, 19,… is 53. Is he correct? Explain.

3. Find the missing terms in each sequence.

    a) 8, 12, _____, 20   b) 11, _____, _____, 26

    c) 15, _____, _____, 24, _____   d) 59, _____, _____, _____, 71

4.

Term Number	Term
1	13
2	15
3	18
4	19
5	21

Term Number	Term
1	25
2	29
3	34
4	37
5	41

Each T-Table was made by adding a number repeatedly.

Find and correct any mistakes in the tables.

5. Rita made an ornament using a hexagon (shaded figure), pentagons (dotted) and triangles.

    a) How many pentagons does she need to make 7 ornaments?

    b) Rita used 6 hexagons to make ornaments.
       How many triangles and pentagons did she use?

    c) Rita used 36 pentagons. How many triangles did she use?

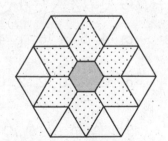

6. A newborn Siberian Tiger cub weighs 1 300 g. It gains 100 g a day.
   A newborn baby weighs 3 300 g. It gains 200 g every week.

    a) A cub and a baby are born on the same day. Who weighs more after…

        i) 2 weeks?   ii) 6 weeks?

    b) After how many weeks would the cub and the baby have the same weight?

jump math
MULTIPLYING POTENTIAL

Patterns & Algebra 1

Gene makes a **repeating pattern** using blocks:

This is the core of Gene's pattern.

The **core** of a pattern is the part that repeats.

----

1. Circle the core of the following patterns. The first one is done for you:

a) 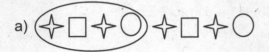   b)

c)    d)

e) Z G H H U Z G H H U Z   f) 1 2 4 8 1 2 4 8 1 2 4 8 1 2 4

g) 9 3 3 9 8 9 3 3 9 8 9   h)

i) ▼ △ ▽ ▼ ▼ △ ▽ ▼   j) Z Y Z Z Y Z Z Y Z

2. Circle the core of the pattern. Then continue the pattern:

a) △ □ □ △ □ □ △ ___ ___ ___ ___ ___

b) ◎ △ ◎ ◎ △ ◎ ___ ___ ___ ___ ___

c) 4 5 4 6 1 4 5 4 6 1 ___ ___ ___ ___ ___

d) 2 2 0 2 2 0 2 2 0 2 ___ ___ ___ ___ ___

e) A A C A A C A ___ ___ ___ ___ ___

f) 2 6 2 2 6 2 2 6 2 2 6 ___ ___ ___ ___ ___ ___

3. Draw your own repeating pattern in the space below:

1. Angela makes a repeating pattern using blue (**B**) and yellow (**Y**) blocks.
   The box shows the core of her pattern. Continue the pattern by writing Bs and Ys:

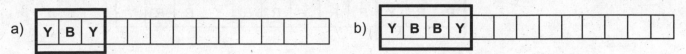

a) | Y | B | Y |

b) | Y | B | B | Y |

2. Joseph tried to continue the pattern in a box. Did he continue the pattern correctly?
   HINT: Shade the yellows (Y) if it helps.

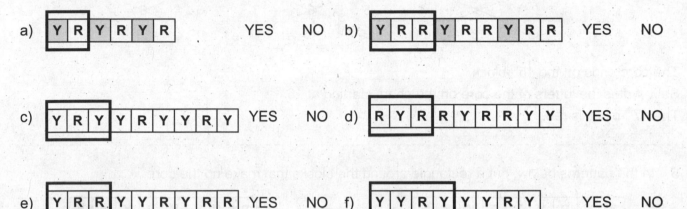

a) Y R Y R Y R   YES   NO

b) Y R R Y R R Y R R   YES   NO

c) Y R Y Y R Y Y R Y   YES   NO

d) R Y R R Y R R Y Y   YES   NO

e) Y R R Y Y R Y R R   YES   NO

f) Y Y R Y Y Y R Y   YES   NO

3. For each pattern below, say whether the blocks in the rectangle are the <u>core</u> of the pattern.

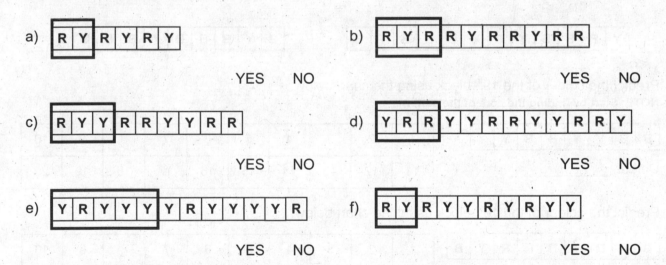

a) R Y R Y R Y   YES   NO

b) R Y R R Y R R Y R R   YES   NO

c) R Y Y R R Y Y R R   YES   NO

d) Y R R Y Y R R Y Y R R Y   YES   NO

e) Y R Y Y Y Y R Y Y Y Y R   YES   NO

f) R Y R Y Y R Y R Y Y   YES   NO

4. Draw a rectangle around the core of the pattern:

a)

b)

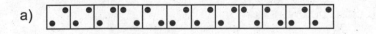

c) → → ↑ ← → → ↑ ← → → ↑

d) ○ △ △ ○ ○ △ △ ○

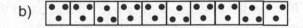

Sally wants to predict the colour of the 17th block in the pattern. First she finds the core of the pattern.

| R | R | Y | R | R | Y | R | R | Y | R | R | Y |

The core is 3 blocks long. Sally marks every <u>third</u> number on a hundreds chart.

Each X shows the position of a block where the core ends:

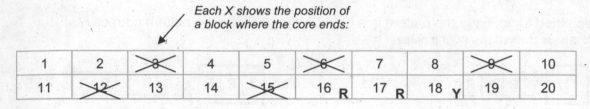

1	2	✗3	4	5	✗6	7	8	✗9	10
11	✗12	13	14	✗15	16 R	17 R	18 Y	19	20

The core ends on the 15th block.

Sally writes the letters of the core on the chart, starting at 16.

The 17th block is red.

---

5. In the patterns below, put a rectangle around the blocks that make up the core.

a) | Y | Y | B | Y | Y | B | Y | Y | B |

b) | Y | B | Y | Y | Y | B | Y | Y | Y |

c) | B | Y | Y | B | B | Y | Y | B | B | Y | Y |

d) | B | B | Y | B | B | B | Y | B |

e) | Y | B | B | B | Y | B | Y | B | B | B | Y | B |

f) | B | Y | B | B | B | Y | B | B | B | Y |

6. Predict the colour of the 19th block using the chart below:

    NOTE: Start by finding the core of the pattern.

| B | B | Y | Y | B | B | Y | Y |

Colour: _____

1	2	3	4	5	6	7	8	9	10
11	12	13	14	15	16	17	18	19	20

7. Predict the colour of the 18th block using the chart below:

| B | R | R | Y | B | R | R | Y | B |

Colour: _____

1	2	3	4	5	6	7	8	9	10
11	12	13	14	15	16	17	18	19	20

8. Predict the colour of the 16th block using the chart below:

| B | R | B | Y | R | B | R | B | Y | R |

Colour: _____

1	2	3	4	5	6	7	8	9	10
11	12	13	14	15	16	17	18	19	20

9. Draw a box around the core of the pattern and predict the colour of the 29th block using the chart below:

Y	B	R	R	Y	B	R	Y	B

Colour: _____

1	2	3	4	5	6	7	8	9	10
11	12	13	14	15	16	17	18	19	20
21	22	23	24	25	26	27	28	29	30

TEACHER: Your students will need a copy of a hundreds chart from the Teacher's Guide.

 10.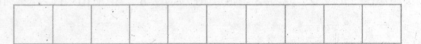

Megan made a pattern with 37 stickers between her bed and her window.
The two suns are next to her bed. Which sticker is next to her window?

11. Design a repeating pattern that uses four colours and has a core that is ten squares long:

What is the colour of the 97th square? How do you know?

12. a) What is the 15th coin in this pattern? Explain how you know.

   b) What is the total value of the first 20 coins?

BONUS
13.

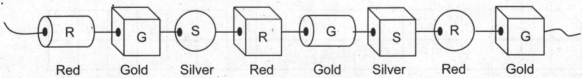

Red   Gold   Silver   Red   Gold   Silver   Red   Gold

Describe the 25th bead in this Christmas tree decoration.

14. For each pattern below, draw a picture of what the 52nd column would look like in the box provided:

   HINT: Look at the patterns in each row separately.

   a) 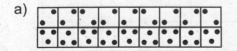   b)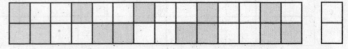

Jacqui is on a bicycle tour 300 km from home. She can cycle 75 km each day.

If she starts riding towards home on Tuesday morning,
how far away from home will she be by Thursday evening?

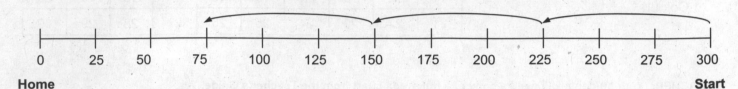

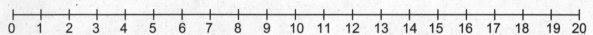

Home   **Start**

On Thursday evening, she will be 75 km from home.

---

1. On Wednesday morning Blair's campsite is 18 km from Tea Lake.
    He plans to hike 5 km towards the lake each day.

    How far from the lake will he be on Friday evening? _____

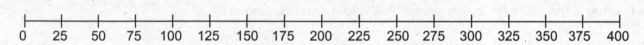

2. On Saturday morning, Samantha is 400 km from her home.
    She can cycle 75 km each day.

    How far from home will she be on Tuesday evening? _____

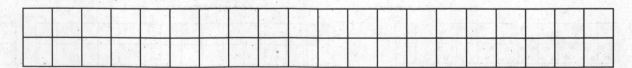

 Draw and label a number line in the grid to solve the problem.

3. 15 L of water drains out of a 90 L tank each minute.

    How much water will be left after 5 minutes?

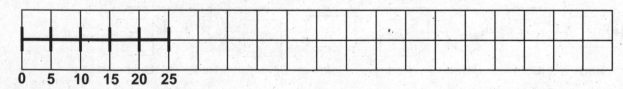

4. Brenda is 70 km from home.

    She can cycle towards home 15 km an hour.

    How far from home will she be in 3 hours?

PA6-10: Number Lines (continued)

5. A grade six class is on a field trip 250 km from home.

    Their bus travels at a speed of 75 km each hour.

    How far from home will they be after 3 hours?

6. Paul plants 5 trees in a row.

    The nearest tree is 5 metres from his house. The farthest tree is 17 metres from his house.

    The trees are equally spaced.

    How far apart are the trees?

    HINT: Put Paul's house at zero on the number line.

7. Michael's house is 18 metres from the ocean.

    He is sleeping in a chair 3 metres away from his house (toward the ocean).

    The tide rises 5 metres every hour. How long will it take before his feet get wet?

8. Robert's bookcase has 5 shelves.

    The top shelf is 150 cm above the floor and the bottom shelf is 30 cm above the floor.

    How far apart are the shelves?

9. Aaron is training for football.

    He runs 5 metres forward and 2 metres back every 4 seconds.

    How far from where he started will he be after 16 seconds?

PA6-11: Lowest Common Multiples

The multiples of 2 and 3 are marked with Xs on the number lines below:

multiples of 2:
0 1 2 3 4 5 6 7 8 9 10 11 12 13 14 15 16

multiples of 3:
0 1 2 3 4 5 6 7 8 9 10 11 12 13 14 15 16

0 is a multiple of every number

The **lowest common multiple** (**LCM**) of 2 and 3 is 6: 6 is the least non-zero number that 2 and 3 both divide into evenly.

---

1. Mark the multiples of the given numbers on the number lines. What is the lowest common multiple of the pair?

   a) 0 1 2 3 4 5 6 7 8 9 10 11 12 13 14 15 16

   3:

   4:
   0 1 2 3 4 5 6 7 8 9 10 11 12 13 14 15 16   LCM = _____

   b) 0 1 2 3 4 5 6 7 8 9 10 11 12 13 14 15 16

   4:

   6:
   0 1 2 3 4 5 6 7 8 9 10 11 12 13 14 15 16   LCM = _____

2. Find the lowest common multiple of each pair of numbers. The first one has been done for you:
   HINT: Count up by the largest number until you find a number that both numbers divide into with no remainder.

   a) 3 and 5   b) 4 and 10   c) 3 and 9   d) 2 and 6

   3: 3, 6, 9, 12, **15**, 18

   5: 5, 10, **15**, 20

   LCM = __15__   LCM = _____   LCM = _____   LCM = _____

   e) 2 and 10   f) 3 and 6   g) 3 and 12   h) 4 and 8   i) 8 and 10

   j) 5 and 15   k) 6 and 10   l) 3 and 10   m) 6 and 8   n) 6 and 9

3. Paul visits the library every <u>fourth</u> day in January (beginning on January 4th).
   Werda visits every <u>sixth</u> day (beginning on January 6th).
   Nigel visits every <u>8</u>th day (beginning on January 8th).

   On what day of the month will they all visit the library together?

Patterns & Algebra 1

PA6-12: Describing and Creating Patterns

In the first sequence, each number is greater than the one before it.
The sequence is always **increasing**:   7   8   10   15   21

In the second sequence, each number is less than the one before it.
The sequence is always **decreasing**:   25   23   18   11   8

----

1. Find the amount by which the sequence <u>increases</u> or <u>decreases</u>. Write a number in the circle, with a
   + sign if the sequence increases, and a **−** sign if it decreases. The first one has been done for you:

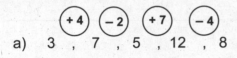

a) 3 , 7 , 5 , 12 , 8

b) 1 , 5 , 4 , 8 , 3

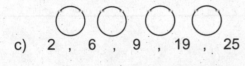

c) 2 , 6 , 9 , 19 , 25

d) 4 , 8 , 7 , 1 , 10

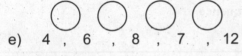

e) 4 , 6 , 8 , 7 , 12

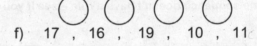

f) 17 , 16 , 19 , 10 , 11

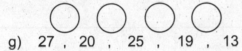

g) 27 , 20 , 25 , 19 , 13

h) 58 , 61 , 54 , 62 , 57

2. Match each sequence with the sentence that describes it. This sequence ....

a) **A** ... increases by 5 each time.
    B ... increases by different amounts.

b) **A** ... decreases by different amounts.
    B ... decreases by the same amount.

____   9 , 13 , 19 , 23 , 25

____   21 , 20 , 18 , 15 , 11

____   8 , 13 , 18 , 23 , 28

____   13 , 10 , 7 , 4 , 1

BONUS

c) **A** ... increases by 5 each time.
    B ... decreases by different amounts.
    C ... increases by different amounts.

d) **A** ... increases and decreases.
    B ... increases by the same amount.
    C ... decreases by different amounts.
    D ... decreases by the same amount.

____   18 , 23 , 29 , 33 , 35

____   27 , 24 , 20 , 19 , 16

____   24 , 29 , 34 , 39 , 44

____   31 , 29 , 25 , 13 , 9

____   10 , 14 , 9 , 6 , 5

____   18 , 16 , 14 , 12 , 10

____   8 , 11 , 14 , 17 , 20

Patterns & Algebra 1

3. Write a rule for each pattern (use the words <u>add</u> or <u>subtract</u>, and say what number the pattern starts with):

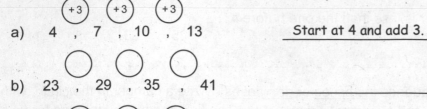

a)   4 , 7 , 10 , 13   Start at 4 and add 3. _____

b)   23 , 29 , 35 , 41   _____

c)   28 , 25 , 22 , 19   _____

d)   53 , 48 , 43 , 38   _____

4. Write a rule for each pattern:
   NOTE: One sequence doesn't have a rule – see if you can find this sequence.

a) 9 , 14 , 19 , 24   _____

b) 27 , 19 , 11 , 3   _____

c) 39 , 31 , 27 , 14 , 9   _____

d) 81 , 85 , 89 , 93   _____

5. Describe each pattern as <u>increasing</u>, <u>decreasing</u> or <u>repeating</u>:

a) 1 , 3 , 6 , 9 , 12 , 15 _____   b) 2 , 8 , 9 , 2 , 8 , 9 _____

c) 29 , 27 , 25 , 23 , 22 _____   d) 2 , 6 , 10 , 14 , 17 _____

e) 3 , 9 , 4 , 3 , 9 , 4 _____   f) 61 , 56 , 51 , 46 , 41 _____

6. Write the first five terms in the pattern:

   a) Start at 38 and add 4.   b) Start at 67 and subtract 6.   c) Start at 98 and add 7.

7. Create an increasing number pattern. Write the rule for your pattern.
   Do the same for a decreasing number pattern.

8. Create a repeating pattern using: a) letters   b) shapes   c) numbers

9. Create a pattern and ask a friend to find the rule for your pattern.

TEACHER: Review ordinal numbers before beginning this page.

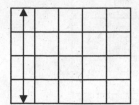

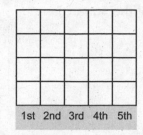

1st 2nd 3rd 4th 5th

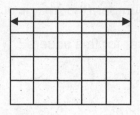

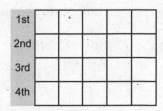
1st
2nd
3rd
4th

Columns run up and down.

Columns are numbered left to right (in this exercise).

Rows run sideways.

Rows are numbered from top to bottom (in this exercise).

---

1. Shade ...

a)

2	6	10
10	14	18
18	22	26

the 2nd row

b)

2	6	10
10	14	18
18	22	26

the 1st column

c)

2	6	10
10	14	18
18	22	26

the 3rd column

d)

2	6	10
10	14	18
18	22	26

the diagonals
(one is shaded here)

2. Describe the pattern in the numbers you see in each chart below:
   NOTE: You should use the words "rows", "columns", and "diagonals" in your answer.

a)

1	3	5
5	7	9
9	11	13

b)

6	12	18	24
12	18	24	30
18	24	30	36
24	30	36	42

c)

16	20	24	28
12	16	20	24
8	12	16	20
4	8	12	16

3. Make up your own pattern and describe it:

4. Place the letters X and Y so that each row and each column has two Xs and two Ys in it:

5. a) Which row of the chart has a decreasing pattern (looking left to right)?

   b) Which column has a repeating pattern?

   c) Write pattern rules for the first and second column.

   d) Describe the relationship between the numbers in the third and fourth columns.

   e) Describe one other pattern in the chart.

   f) Name a row or column that does not appear to have any pattern.

0	4	8	6	2
5	6	7	5	9
10	8	6	4	2
15	10	5	3	9
20	12	4	2	2

1. In a magic square, the numbers in each row, column, and diagonal all add up to the same number (the "magic number" for the square):

   What is the magic number for this square? _____

2	9	4
7	5	3
6	1	8

2. Complete the magic squares:

   a)
2		6
9	5	
4	3	

   b)
	9	
10	5	12

   c)
		10
	12	
14		18

3. Here are some number pyramids:

   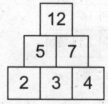
   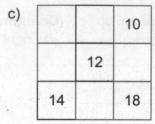

   Can you find the rule by which the patterns in the pyramids were made? Describe it here:

4. Using the rule you described in Question 3, find the missing numbers:

   a) [ ] over [2][4]

   b) [ ] over [1][7]

   c) [ ] over [9][2]

   d) [7] over [4][ ]

   e) [10] over [ ][6]

   f)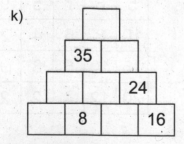

   g)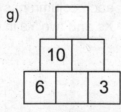

   h)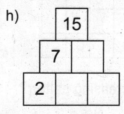

   i)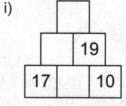

   j)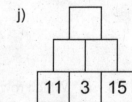

   k)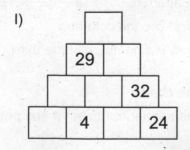

   l)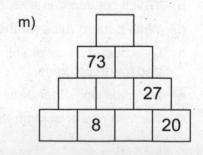

   m)

PA6-15: Finding Rules for T-tables – Part I

Andre makes a garden path using 6 triangular stones for every 1 square stone.

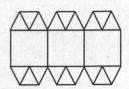

He writes an equation that shows how to calculate the number of triangles from the number of squares:

squares × 6 = triangles

or (for short):   **6 × s = t**

Squares (s)	6 × s = t	Triangles (t)
1	6 × [1] = 6	6
2	6 × [2] = 12	12
3	6 × [3] = 18	18

1. Each chart represents a different design for a path. Complete the charts:

a)

Squares (s)	4 × s = t	Triangles (t)
1	4 × [1] = 4	4
2	4 × [ ] = 8	
3	4 × [ ] = 12	

b)

Squares (s)	3 × s = t	Triangles (t)
1	3 × [ ] = 3	
2	3 × [ ] = 6	
3	3 × [ ] = 9	

2. Write a rule that tells you how to calculate the number of triangles from the number of squares:

a)

Squares	Triangles
1	4
2	8
3	12

b)

Squares	Triangles
1	5
2	10
3	15

c)

Squares	Triangles
1	2
2	4
3	6

d)

Squares	Triangles
1	6
2	12
3	18

3. Wendy makes broaches using squares (s), rectangles (r), and triangles (t). Complete the chart. Write an equation (such as **4 × s = t**) for each design:

a)

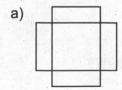

Squares (s)	Rectangles (r)
1	
2	
3	

b)

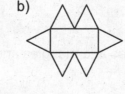

Rectangles (r)	Triangles (t)
1	
2	
3	

jump math
MULTIPLYING POTENTIAL.

Patterns & Algebra 1

c)

Squares (s)	Rectangles (r)

d)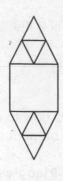

Squares (s)	Triangles (t)

e)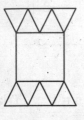

Squares (s)	Triangles (t)

f)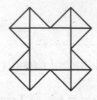

Squares (s)	Triangles (t)

4. Wendy has 39 triangles.

   Does she have enough triangles to make 7 broaches using the design here?

   How can you tell without making a chart?

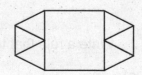

5. Create a design using squares (s) and triangles (t) to go with each equation:

   a) $6 \times s = t$

   b) $5 \times s = t$

6. Create a design with squares and triangles and then write an equation for your design:

In the auditorium, the number of chairs in each row is always 4 greater than the row number.

Kelly writes an equation that shows how to calculate the number of chairs from the row number:

row number + 4 = number of chairs (or r + 4 = c for short)

Row 1
Row 2
Row 3

Row	r + 4 = c	Chairs
1	1 + 4 = 5	5
2	2 + 4 = 6	6
3	3 + 4 = 7	7

---

7. Each chart represents a different arrangement of chairs. Complete the charts:

a)

Row	r + 6 = c	Chairs
1	1 + 6 = 7	7
2	+ 6 =	
3	+ 6 =	

b)

Row	r + 9 = c	Chairs
1	+ 9 =	
2	+ 9 =	
3	+ 9 =	

8. Say what number you must add to the row number to get the number of chairs.
    Write an equation using **r** for the row number and **c** for the number of chairs:

a)

Row	Chairs
1	5
2	6
3	7

Add 4

$r + 4 = c$

b)

Row	Chairs
1	8
2	9
3	10

c)

Row	Chairs
1	9
2	10
3	11

d)

Row	Chairs
7	12
8	13
9	14

9. Complete the charts. Then, in the box provided, write an equation for each arrangement of chairs:

a)

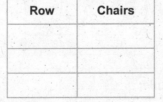

Row	Chairs

b)

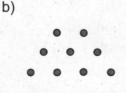

Row	Chairs

10. Apply the given rule to the numbers in the input column. Write your answer in the output column:

a)

INPUT	OUTPUT
1	
2	
3	

Rule:

Add 4 to the input.

b)

INPUT	OUTPUT
5	
6	
7	

Rule:

Subtract 4 from the input.

c)

INPUT	OUTPUT
3	
5	
6	

Rule:

Multiply the input by 6.

d)

INPUT	OUTPUT
32	
8	
40	

Rule:

Divide each input by 4.

e)

INPUT	OUTPUT
18	
19	
20	

Rule:

Add 10 to the input.

f)

INPUT	OUTPUT
4	
5	
6	

Rule:

Multiply the input by 8.

11. For each chart, give a rule that tells you how to make the output numbers from the input numbers.

a)

INPUT	OUTPUT
2	6
3	7
4	8

Rule:

b)

INPUT	OUTPUT
3	8
5	10
7	12

Rule:

c)

INPUT	OUTPUT
1	7
2	14
3	21

Rule:

d)

INPUT	OUTPUT
3	15
2	10
1	5

Rule:

e)

INPUT	OUTPUT
2	16
4	32
6	48

Rule:

f)

INPUT	OUTPUT
19	16
15	12
21	18

Rule:

1. Complete the T-table for each pattern.
   Then write a rule that tells you how to calculate the second number from the first number.

a)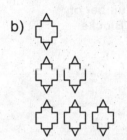

Number of Vertical Lines	Number of Horizontal Lines

Rule: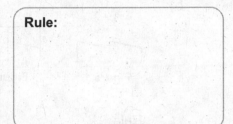

b)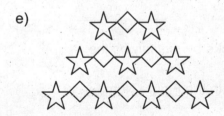

Number of Crosses	Number of Triangles

Rule:

c)

Number of Suns	Number of Moons

Rule: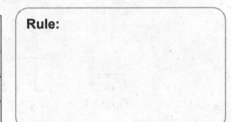

d)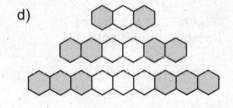

Number of Light Hexagons	Number of Dark Hexagons

Rule:

e)

Number of Diamonds	Number of Stars

Rule:

2. Make a T-table and write a rule for the number of hexagons and triangles:

Figure 1   Figure 2   Figure 3

3. How many triangles are needed for 9 hexagons in the pattern in Question 2? How do you know?

Fill in the chart and write a rule for the number of blocks in each figure, as shown in part a).

1. a)

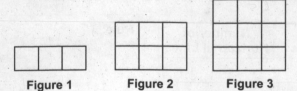

Figure 1   Figure 2   Figure 3

Rule: __3 × Figure Number__

Figure Number	Number of Blocks
1	
2	
3	

b)

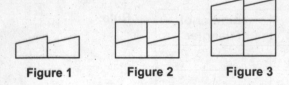

Figure 1   Figure 2   Figure 3

Rule: _____

Figure Number	Number of Blocks

c)

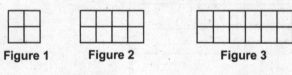

Figure 1   Figure 2   Figure 3

Rule: _____

Figure Number	Number of Blocks

d)

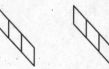 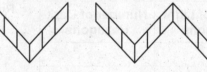 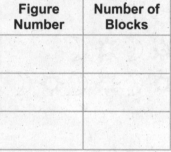

Figure 1   Figure 2   Figure 3

Rule: _____

Figure Number	Number of Blocks

> In each example above, you can find the **total number of blocks** by *multiplying* the **Figure Number** by the **number of blocks in the first figure**.
>
> In such cases, **the number of blocks** is said to vary <u>directly</u> with the <u>Figure Number</u>.

2. Circle the sequences where the number of blocks varies <u>directly</u> with the Figure Number:

a)

Figure Number	Number of Blocks
1	3
2	6
3	9

b)

Figure Number	Number of Blocks
1	4
2	7
3	10

c)

Figure Number	Number of Blocks
1	6
2	12
3	18

d)

Figure Number	Number of Blocks
1	5
2	10
3	16

1. In each pattern below, the number of *shaded* blocks increases <u>directly</u> with the Figure Number.
   The *total* number of blocks, however, <u>does not</u> increase directly.

       i)   Write a rule for the number of *shaded* blocks in each sequence.

       ii)   Write a rule for the *total number* of blocks in each sequence.

a)

Figure 1   **Figure 2**   **Figure 3**

Rule for the number of shaded blocks:

2 × Figure Number

Rule for the total number of blocks:

2 × Figure Number + 1

b)

Figure 1   **Figure 2**   **Figure 3**

Rule for the number of shaded blocks:

_____

Rule for the total number of blocks:

_____

c)

Figure 1   **Figure 2**   **Figure 3**

Rule for the number of shaded blocks:

_____

Rule for the total number of blocks:

_____

d)

Figure 1   **Figure 2**   **Figure 3**

Rule for the number of shaded blocks:

_____

Rule for the total number of blocks:

_____

e)   Rule for the number of shaded blocks:

_____

Rule for the total number of blocks:

_____

 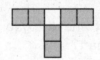 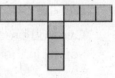

Figure 1   **Figure 2**   **Figure 3**

2. Draw or build a sequence of figures that might go with the following tables.
   Shade the part of each figure that varies directly with the Figure Number:

a)

Figure Number	Number of Blocks
1	5
2	7
3	9

b)

Figure Number	Number of Blocks
1	6
2	10
3	14

c)

Figure Number	Number of Blocks
1	7
2	10
3	13

1. Fill in the chart using the rule.

a) Rule: Multiply by 4 and add 3

INPUT	OUTPUT
1	
2	
3	

Gap: _____

b) Rule: Multiply by 2 and add 3

INPUT	OUTPUT
1	
2	
3	

Gap: _____

c) Rule: Multiply by 5 and add 4

INPUT	OUTPUT
1	
2	
3	

Gap: _____

d) Rule: Multiply by 10 and add 1

INPUT	OUTPUT
1	
2	
3	

Gap: _____

e) Compare the **gap** in each pattern above to the rule for the pattern. What do you notice?

_____

_____

2. For each pattern below, make a T-table as shown.

    Fill in the total number of blocks (shaded and unshaded) and the gap.

    Can you predict what the gap will be for each pattern before you fill in the chart?

Figure Number	Number of Blocks
1	
2	
3	

Figure 1

Figure 2

Figure 3

Figure 1

Figure 2

Figure 3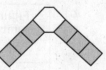

Figure 1

Figure 2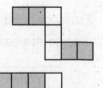

Figure 3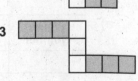

Can you write a rule for each pattern that tells how to find the number of blocks from the figure number?

In the T-table shown here, the output is calculated from the input by two operations:

To find the rule:

INPUT	OUTPUT
1	5
2	8
3	11

Step 1:
Find the step (or gap) between the numbers in the OUTPUT column.

INPUT	INPUT x GAP	OUTPUT	
1	·	5	3
2		8	3
3		11	

Step 2:
Multiply the INPUT numbers by the gap.

INPUT	INPUT x GAP	OUTPUT	
1	3	5	3
2	6	8	3
3	9	11	

Step 3:
What must you add to each number in the second column?

INPUT	INPUT x GAP	OUTPUT	
1	3	5	3
2	6	8	3
3	9	11	

Add 2

Step 4:
Write a rule for the T-table – **Rule:** _Multiply the input by 3 and add 2_

----

1. Use the steps above to find the rule that tells you how to calculate the OUTPUT from the INPUT:

a)

INPUT	INPUT x GAP	OUTPUT
1		9
2		13
3		17

Add _____

Rule: Multiply by _____ then add _____.

b)

INPUT	INPUT x GAP	OUTPUT
1		3
2		5
3		7

Add _____

Rule: Multiply by _____ then add _____.

c)

INPUT	INPUT x GAP	OUTPUT
1		7
2		10
3		13

Add _____

Rule: Multiply by _____ then add _____.

d)

INPUT	INPUT x GAP	OUTPUT
1		6
2		8
3		10

Add _____

Rule: Multiply by _____ then add _____.

jump math
MULTIPLYING POTENTIAL

Patterns & Algebra 1

2. Write a rule that tells you how to calculate the OUTPUT from the INPUT:

a)

INPUT	INPUT x GAP	OUTPUT
1		9
2		14
3		19

Multiply by _____ then add _____.

b)

INPUT	INPUT x GAP	OUTPUT
1		12
2		18
3		24

Multiply by _____ then add _____.

c)

INPUT	INPUT x GAP	OUTPUT
1		6
2		10
3		14

Multiply by _____ then add _____.

d)

INPUT	INPUT x GAP	OUTPUT
1		6
2		11
3		16

Multiply by _____ then add _____.

3. Write the rule that tells you how to calculate the OUTPUT from the INPUT:
NOTE: In this case you will have to subtract rather than add.

a)

INPUT	INPUT x GAP	OUTPUT
1		4
2		9
3		14

Multiply by _____ then subtract _____.

b)

INPUT	INPUT x GAP	OUTPUT
1		1
2		4
3		7

Multiply by _____ then subtract _____.

c)

INPUT	INPUT x GAP	OUTPUT
1		2
2		6
3		10

Multiply by _____ then subtract _____.

d)

INPUT	INPUT x GAP	OUTPUT
1		5
2		11
3		17

Multiply by _____ then subtract _____.

4. Write a rule that tells you how to make the Output from the Input:
    Each rule may involve either one or two operations.

a)

Input	Output
1	2
2	7
3	12
4	17

Rule:

b)

Input	Output
1	3
2	9
3	15
4	21

Rule:

c)

Input	Output
1	5
2	6
3	7
4	8

Rule:

d)

Input	Output
1	7
2	9
3	11
4	13

Rule:

e)

Input	Output
0	4
1	8
2	12
3	16

Rule:

f)

Input	Output
1	4
2	8
3	12
4	16

Rule:

BONUS

5. Find the rule by guessing and checking.

a)

Input	Output
5	27
6	32
7	37
8	42

Rule:

b)

Input	Output
4	7
5	9
6	11
7	13

Rule:

c)

Input	Output
57	63
58	64
59	65
60	66

Rule:

d)

Input	Output
2	7
4	13
6	19
8	25

Rule:

e)

Input	Output
10	31
9	28
3	10
1	4

Rule:

f)

Input	Output
8	13
4	5
3	3
7	11

Rule:

PA6-21: Applying Rules for Patterns

1. For each, draw Figure 4 and fill in the T-table.
   Then write a rule that tells you how to calculate the input from the output:

a)

    1   2   3   4

Figure	Number of Triangles
1	
2	
3	
4	

Rule for T-table: _____

Use your rule to predict how many triangles will be needed for Figure 9: _____

b)

1   2   3   4

Figure	Number of Line Segments
1	
2	
3	
4	

Rule for T-table: _____

Use your rule to predict the number of line segments in Figure 11: _____

c)

1   2   3   4

Figure	Number of Squares
1	
2	
3	
4	

Rule for T-table: _____

Use your rule to predict the number of squares needed for Figure 10: _____

d)

1   2   3   4

Figure	Perimeter
1	
2	
3	
4	

Rule for T-table: _____

Use your rule to predict the perimeter of Figure 23: _____

NS6-1: Introduction to Place Value

1. Write the place value of the underlined digit.

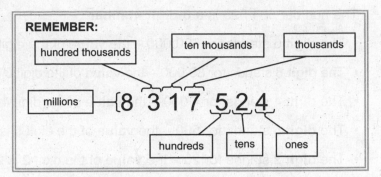

REMEMBER:

a) 56 2<u>3</u>6 → tens

b) <u>1</u> 956 336

c) 8 <u>2</u>56 601

d) 6 453 <u>1</u>56

e) 7 103 25<u>6</u>

f) 2 5<u>8</u>9 143

g) 9<u>2</u>3 156

2. Give the place value of the number 5 in each of the numbers below.
   HINT: First underline the 5 in each question.

a) 35 689

b) 5 308 603

c) 36 905

d) 215

e) 2 542

f) 3 451 628

g) 43 251

h) 152 776

i) 1 543 001

3. You can also write numbers using a place value chart.

Example:

4 672 953 would be:

millions	hundred thousands	ten thousands	thousands	hundreds	tens	ones
4	6	7	2	9	5	3

Write the following numbers into the place value chart.

	millions	hundred thousands	ten thousands	thousands	hundreds	tens	ones
a) 2 316 953	2	3	1	6	9	5	3
b) 62 507							
c) 5 604 891							
d) 1 399							
e) 17							
f) 998 260							

jump math
MULTIPLYING POTENTIAL

Number Sense 1

The number 684 523 is a **6-digit number**.

- The **digit** 6 stands for 600 000 – the **value** of the digit 6 is 600 000
- The **digit** 8 stands for 80 000 – the **value** of the digit 8 is 80 000
- The **digit** 4 stands for 4 000 – the **value** of the digit 4 is 4 000
- The **digit** 5 stands for 500 – the **value** of the digit 5 is 500
- The **digit** 2 stands for 20 – the **value** of the digit 2 is 20
- The **digit** 3 stands for 3 – the **value** of the digit 3 is 3

----

1. Write the **value** of each digit.

a)

| 6 | 5 | 4 | 8 | 7 | 2 |

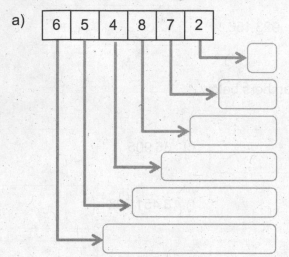

b)

| 1 | 2 | 8 | 5 | 3 | 7 |

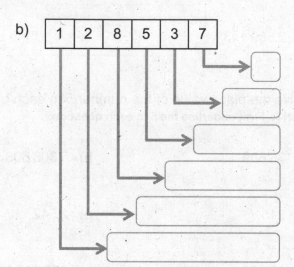

2. What does the digit 7 stand for in each number? The first one is done for you.

a)   8 476

70

b)   38 725

c)   93 726

d)   730 025

e)   7 250

f)   64 297

g)   43 075

h)   382 457

3. Fill in the blanks.

a) In the number 4 523, the <u>digit</u> 5 stands for _____ .

b) In the number 34 528, the <u>digit</u> 3 stands for _____ .

c) In the number 420 583, the <u>value</u> of the digit 8 is _____ .

d) In the number 75 320, the <u>value</u> of the digit 7 is _____ .

e) In the number 723 594, the digit _____ is in the <u>ten thousands place</u>.

NS6-3: Reading and Writing Large Numbers

1. Say whether the underlined numbers represent **thousands** or **millions**.

   a) <u>327</u> 510 210

   _____millions_____

   b) 216 <u>772</u> 015

   _____

   c) 879 <u>054</u> 815

   _____

   d) <u>65</u> 321 879

   _____

Correct spelling for the tens place:	
ten	sixty
twenty	seventy
thirty	eighty
forty	ninety
fifty	

2. Write the value of the underlined digits.

   a) <u>375</u> 231 872   <u>three hundred seventy-five million</u>

   b) 287 <u>036</u> 253 _____

   c) <u>79</u> 253 812 _____

   d) 3 <u>770</u> 823 _____

3. Write numerals for the numbers.

   a) Two hundred eighty-three million, four hundred twenty-two thousand

   b) Seventy-three million, fifty-seven thousand, one hundred four

   c) Nine hundred seven million, four hundred three thousand, twenty-one

4. Write number words for the numerals.

   a) 275 381 210

   b) 89 023 100

   c) 998 325 593

5. Write the numbers in the chart in words. (Note: **mya** means millions of years ago.)

   Dinosaurs evolve   *Birds evolve*   *Dinosaurs become extinct*

Triassic Period	Jurassic Period	Cretaceous Period

   248 mya   214 mya   206 mya   65 mya

6. Complete each sentence with a written number in the hundred thousands or the hundred millions.

   a) A small city can have a population of…

   b) A large country can have a population of…

7. Write the numerals in the chart in words.

Planet	Distance from Sun (km)
Mercury	57 600 000
Venus	107 520 000
Earth	148 640 000

8. **Billions** come after millions.
   The planet Neptune is 4 468 640 000 km from the sun. Write this number in words.

9. Explain how our place value system makes it easy to read and write large numbers.

TEACHER: Model the two kinds of expanded form for your students.

1. Write each number in expanded form.
    (numerals and words).

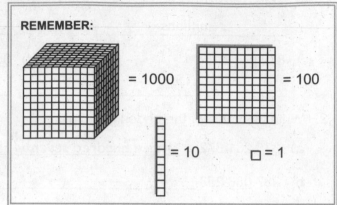

REMEMBER:

= 1000   = 100   = 10   □ = 1

Example:

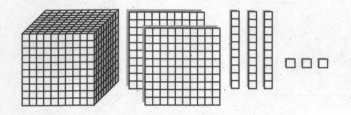

<u> 1 </u> thousands + <u> 2 </u> hundreds + <u> 3 </u> tens + <u> 3 </u> ones = | 1 233 |

a)

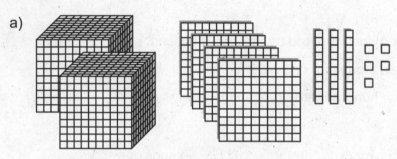

___ thousands + ___ hundreds + ___ tens + ___ ones = [   ]

b)

___ thousands + ___ hundreds + ___ tens + ___ ones = [   ]

c)

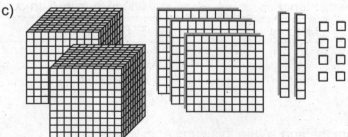

_____ = [   ]

Steps for drawing a thousands block:

Step 1:
Draw a square:

Step 2:
Draw lines from
its 3 vertices:

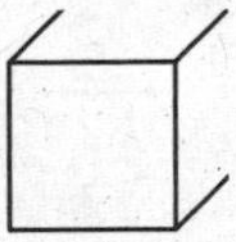

Step 3:
Join the lines:

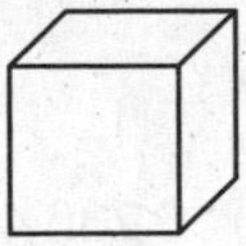

2. Represent the given numbers with the base ten blocks in the place value chart. The first one has been started for you.

	Number	Thousands	Hundreds	Tens	Ones
a)	3 468	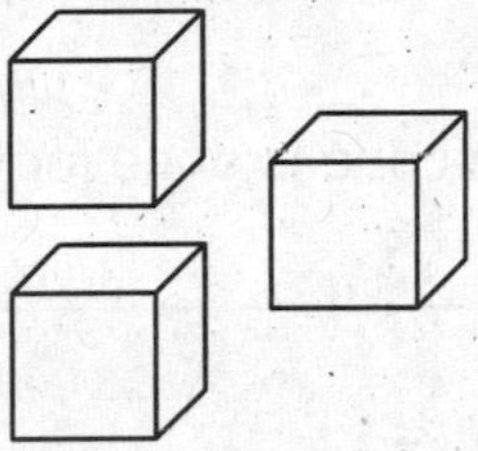	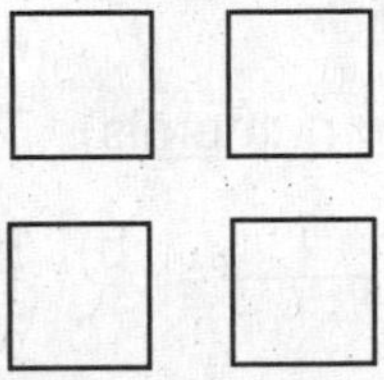		
b)	1 542				
c)	2 609				

3. Write the numbers for the given base ten blocks.

	Thousands	Hundreds	Tens	Ones	Number
a)	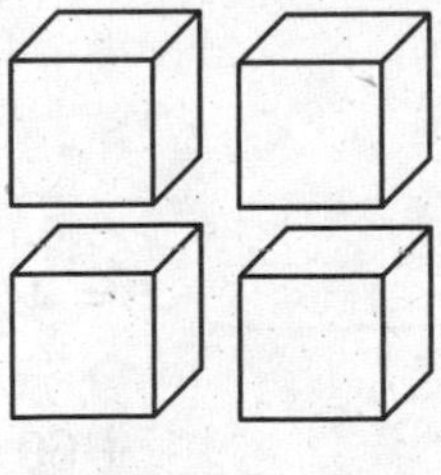	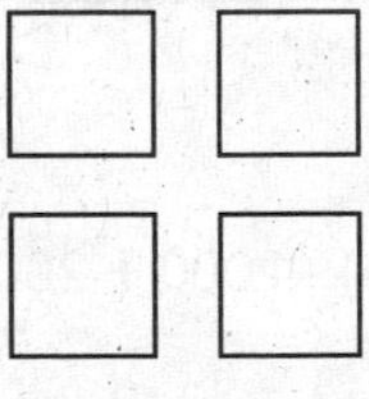	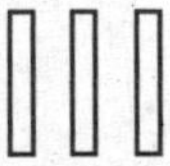		_____
b)	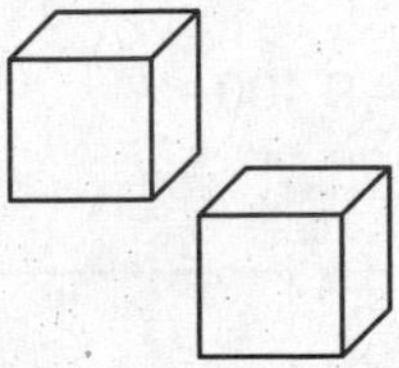	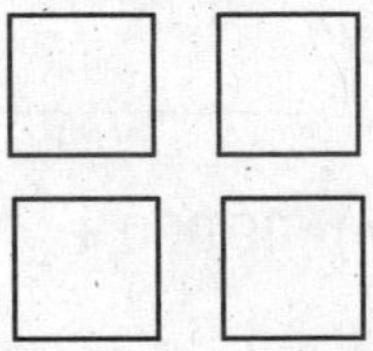	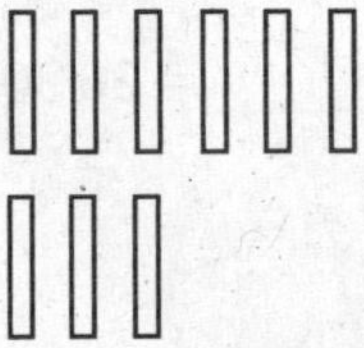		_____

1. Expand the following numbers using <u>numerals</u> and <u>words</u>. The first one is done for you.

    a) 2 536 784 = __2__ millions + __5__ hundred thousands + __3__ ten thousands + __6__ thousands

        + __7__ hundreds + __8__ tens + __4__ ones

    b) 6 235 401 = _____

        _____

    c) 3 056 206 = _____

        _____

2. Write the number in expanded form (using <u>numerals</u>). The first one is done for you.

    a) 72 613 = __70 000 + 2 000 + 600 + 10 + 3__   b) 36 = _____

    c) 526 = _____   d) 12 052 = _____

    e) 2 382 = _____   f) 56 384 = _____

    g) 3 082 385 = _____

3. Write the number for each sum.

    a) 6 000 + 700 + 40 + 7 = _____   b) 800 + 60 + 8 = _____   c) 3 000 + 30 + 2 = _____

    d) 50 000 + 6 000 + 400 + 90 + 3 = _____   e) 10 000 + 6 000 + 200 + 30 + 4 = _____

    f) 30 000 + 2 000 + 500 = _____   g) 90 000 + 3 000 + 600 + 7 = _____

BONUS
    h) 300 000 + 2 000 000 + 5 + 70 000 + 200 = _____

4. Find the missing numbers.

    a) 2 000 + 600 + _____ + 5 = 2 645   b) 4 000 + 200 + _____ + 5 = 4 285

    c) 40 000 + 3 000 + _____ + 10 + 5 = 43 715   d) 80 000 + 5 000 + _____ + 60 + 3 = 85 263

    e) 20 000 + 6 000 + 300 + _____ = 26 302   f) _____ + 400 = 9 400

    g) 6 000 + _____ = 6 080   h) 80 000 + _____ + _____ = 87 005

    i) 300 000 + 90 000 + _____ + _____ = 390 702

5. Write each number in expanded form. Then draw a base ten model.

Example: 3 152 =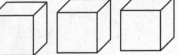

a) 4 354 =

b) 2 604 =

---

6. Represent the number 8 564 in four different ways – by sketching a base ten model, with number words, and in expanded form (2 ways).

Example: 234 – Two hundred thirty-four

234 = 2 hundreds + 3 tens + 4 ones   *expanded form (using number words)*

234 = 200 + 30 + 4   *expanded form (using numerals)*

7. In the number 38 562, what is the sum of the tens digit and the thousands digit?

8. How many two-digit numbers have digits that add to twelve?

9. Using 5 blocks make (or draw) a model of a number such that…

- The number is odd
- There are twice as many thousands blocks as hundreds blocks

10. How many thousands blocks would you need to represent a million?

1. Write the **value** of each digit. Then complete the sentence.

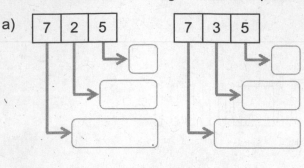   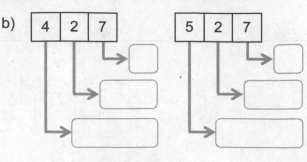

a) | 7 | 2 | 5 | | 7 | 3 | 5 | b) | 4 | 2 | 7 | | 5 | 2 | 7 |

_____ is greater than _____   _____ is greater than _____

2. Circle the pair of digits that are different in each pair of numbers.
   Then write the greater number in the box.

a) 83 7(5)2
   83 7(6)2
   [83 762]

b) 273 605
   272 605
   [ ]

c) 614 852
   614 858
   [ ]

d) 383 250
   483 250
   [ ]

e) 812 349
   813 349
   [ ]

f) 569 274
   579 274
   [ ]

g) 323
   324
   [ ]

h) 195 385
   196 385
   [ ]

3. Read the numbers from left to right. Circle the first pair of digits you find that are different.
   Then write the greater number in the box.

a) 641 5(8)3
   641 5(9)7
   [641 597]

b) 384 207
   389 583
   [ ]

c) 576 986
   603 470
   [ ]

d) 621 492
   621 483
   [ ]

4. The inequality sign '>' in **7 > 5** is read "seven is greater than five."
   The sign '<' **8 < 10** is read "eight is less than ten."
   Write the correct inequality sign in the box.

a) 8 653 [>] 8 486   b) 15 332 [ ] 16 012   c) 9 000 [ ] 7 999

d) 323 728 [ ] 323 729   e) 648 175 [ ] 648 123   f) 72 382 [ ] 8 389

g) 24 489 [ ] 38 950   h) 85 106 [ ] 83 289   i) 1 572 306 [ ] 1 573 306

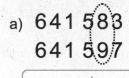 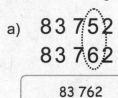

jump math
MULTIPLYING POTENTIAL

Number Sense 1

1. Write "10 more", "10 less", "100 more" or "100 less" in the blanks.

   a) 70 is _____ than 60   b) 500 is _____ than 600

   c) 40 is _____ than 30   d) 100 is _____ than 90

2. Write "100 more", "100 less", "1 000 more", or "1 000 less" in the blanks.

   a) 1 000 is _____ than 2 000   b) 14 000 is _____ than 15 000

   c) 5 900 is _____ than 6 000   d) 70 000 is _____ than 69 000

3. Write "1 000 more", "1 000 less", "10 000 more", or "10 000 less" in the blanks.

   a) 7 000 is _____ than 6 000   b) 13 000 is _____ than 14 000

   c) 40 000 is _____ than 50 000 d) 60 000 is _____ than 50 000

   e) 8 000 is _____ than 7 000   f) 40 000 is _____ than 39 000

4. Write "10 000 more", "10 000 less", "100 000 more", or "100 000 less" in the blanks.

   a) 200 000 is _____ than 100 000   b) 70 000 is _____ than 80 000

   c) 160 000 is _____ than 150 000   d) 400 000 is _____ than 500 000

   e) 190 000 is _____ than 200 000   f) 800 000 is _____ than 900 000

5. Circle the pair of digits that are different. Then fill in the blanks.

   a) 385 237   b) 291 375   c) 143 750
      395 237   291 475   133 750

   385 237 is ___10 000 less___   291 375 is _____   143 750 is _____
   than 395 237.   than 291 475.   than 133 750.

   d) 522 508   e) 96 405   f) 3 752 582
      532 508   96 415   3 751 582

   522 508 is _____   96 405 is _____   3 752 582 is _____
   than 532 508.   than 96 415.   than 3 751 582.

6. Fill in the blanks.

a) _____ is 10 more than 3 782

b) _____ is 100 less than 39 927

c) _____ is 100 more than 3 782

d) _____ is 1 000 less than 15 023

e) _____ is 10 000 more than 287 532

f) _____ is 1 000 less than 23 685

g) _____ is 10 000 more than 8 305

h) _____ is 100 000 more than 4 253

i) _____ is 100 000 less than 273 528

j) _____ is 10 000 less than 178 253

7. Fill in the blanks.

a) $226 + 10 =$ _____

b) $28\,573 + 10 =$ _____

c) $39\,035 + 10 =$ _____

d) $42\,127 + 100 =$ _____

e) $63\,283 + 1\,000 =$ _____

f) $58\,372 + 10\,000 =$ _____

g) $2\,873 - 10 =$ _____

h) $485 - 10 =$ _____

i) $837 - 100 =$ _____

j) $32\,487 - 1\,000 =$ _____

k) $81\,901 - 100 =$ _____

l) $25\,836 - 10\,000 =$ _____

m) $382\,507 + 10\,000 =$ _____

n) $1\,437\,652 - 100\,000 =$ _____

8. Fill in the blanks.

a) $685 +$ _____ $= 695$

b) $302 +$ _____ $= 402$

c) $2\,375 +$ _____ $= 2\,385$

d) $2\,617 +$ _____ $= 2\,717$

e) $43\,210 +$ _____ $= 44\,210$

f) $26\,287 +$ _____ $= 26\,387$

g) $1\,287 -$ _____ $= 1\,187$

h) $6\,325 -$ _____ $= 6\,315$

i) $14\,392 -$ _____ $= 14\,292$

j) $386\,053 -$ _____ $= 376\,053$

k) $1\,260\,053 + 1\,000 =$ _____

BONUS
9. Continue the number patterns.

a) 6 407, 6 417, 6 427, _____ , _____

b) 46 640, 47 640, 48 640, _____ , _____

c) 624 823, 624 833, _____ , 624 853

d) _____ , 28 393, 28 403, 28 413

10. Circle the pair of digits that are different. Then fill in the blanks.

a) 827 325
   827 335

   827 325 is 10
   less than 827 335

b) 382 305
   482 305

   _____ is _____
   greater than _____

c) 925 778
   915 778

   _____ is _____
   less than _____

1. Write the number represented by the base ten materials in each box. Then circle the greater number in each pair.

   HINT: If there is the same number of thousands, count the number of hundreds or tens.

   a) (i)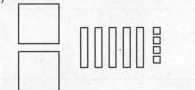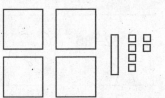

   (ii)

   b) (i)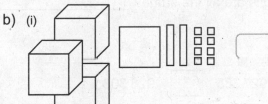

   (ii)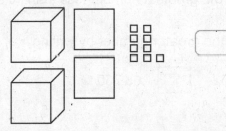

2. Circle the greater number in each pair.

   a) 47 or forty-eight   b) three thousand, five hundred seven or 3508   c) ninety-four or 88

   d) six hundred fifty-five or 662   e) 60 385 or sixty thousand four hundred twenty-five

3. List all the two-digit numbers you can make using the digits provided (using each digit only once). Then circle the greatest one.

   a) 6, 7 and 8   b) 2, 9 and 4   c) 5, 2, and 0

4. Create the greatest possible <u>four-digit</u> number using the digits given. Only use each digit once.

   a) 4, 3, 2, 6 _____   b) 7, 8, 9, 4 _____   c) 0, 4, 1, 2 _____

5. Create the greatest possible number using these digits. Only use each digit once.

   a) 3, 4, 1, 2, 8 _____   b) 2, 8, 9, 1, 5 _____   c) 3, 6, 1, 5, 4 _____

6. Use the digits to create the greatest number, the least number and a number in between.

	Digits	Greatest Number	Number in Between	Least Number
a)	8 5 7 2 1			
b)	2 1 5 3 9			
c)	3 0 1 5 3			

7. Arrange the numbers in order, starting with the <u>least</u> number.

a) 683 759, 693 238, 693 231

b) 473 259, 42 380, 47 832

_____ , _____ , _____   _____ , _____ , _____

c) 385 290, 928 381, 532 135

d) 2 575, 38 258, 195

_____ , _____ , _____   _____ , _____ , _____

8. What is the greatest number less than 10 000 whose digits are all the same? _____

9. Identify the greater number by writing > or <.

a) 63 752 ☐ 63 750

b) 927 385 ☐ 928 303

c) 572 312 ☐ 59 238

d) 1 230 075 ☐ 1 230 123

10.

City	Population
Ottawa	774 072
Hamilton	662 401
Kitchener	414 284

a) Which city has a population greater than 670 000?

_____

b) Write the populations in order from least to greatest.

_____

11. What is the greatest possible number you can create that has …

a) 3 digits? _____   b) 4 digits? _____   c) 5 digits? _____

12. Using the digits 0, 1, 2, 3, 4, create an even number greater than 42 000 and less than 43 000.

13. Using the digits 4, 5, 6, 7, 8, create an odd number greater than 64 000 and less than 68 000.

14. What digit can be substituted for ☐ to make each statement true?

a) 54 ☐ 21 is between 54 348 and 54 519.

b) 76 ☐ 99 is between 76 201 and 76 316.

Nancy has 3 hundreds blocks, 14 tens blocks, and 8 ones blocks.
She exchanges 10 tens blocks for a hundreds block.

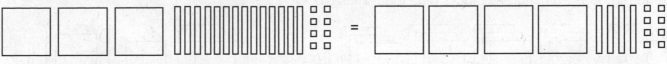

3 hundreds + 14 tens + 8 ones   =   4 hundreds + 4 tens + 8 ones

----

1. Regroup 10 ones as 1 tens block.

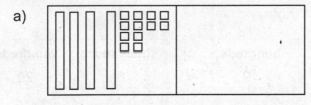   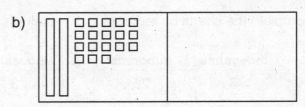

___ tens + ___ ones = ___ tens + ___ ones   ___ tens + ___ ones = ___ tens + ___ ones

2. Exchange ones for tens.

a) 53 ones =___tens + ___ones   b) 85 ones =___tens + ___ones   c) 14 ones =___tens + ___ones

d) 27 ones =___tens + ___ones   e) 32 ones =___tens + ___ones   f) 16 ones =___tens + ___ones

g) 11 ones =___tens + ___ones   h) 82 ones =___tens + ___ones   i) 93 ones =___tens + ___ones

3. Complete the charts by regrouping 10 tens as 1 hundred.

a)

hundreds	tens
7	28
7 + 2 = 9	8

b)

hundreds	tens
6	24

c)

hundreds	tens
3	15

d)

hundreds	tens
6	36

e)

hundreds	tens
8	19

f)

hundreds	tens
2	20

4. Exchange tens for hundreds or ones for tens. The first one has been done for you.

a) 6 hundreds + 7 tens + 19 ones = _6 hundreds + 8 tens + 9 ones_____

b) 2 hundreds + 6 tens + 15 ones = _____

c) 8 hundreds + 28 tens + 9 ones = _____

Rupa has 1 thousands block, 12 hundreds blocks, 1 tens block and 2 ones blocks.

She regroups 10 hundreds blocks as a thousands block.

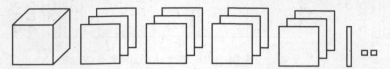 =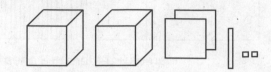

1 thousand + 12 hundreds + 1 ten + 2 ones   =   2 thousands + 2 hundreds + 1 ten + 2 ones

----

5. Complete the charts by regrouping 10 hundreds as 1 thousand.

a)

thousands	hundreds
5	25
5 + 2 = 7	5

b)

thousands	hundreds
3	12

c)

thousands	hundreds
8	20

6. Exchange 10 hundreds for a thousand. The first one has been done for you.

a) 5 thousands + 23 hundreds + 2 tens + 5 ones = __7__ thousands + __3__ hundreds + __2__ tens + __5__ ones

b) 1 thousands + 54 hundreds + 2 tens + 6 ones = ____ thousands + ____ hundreds + ____ tens + ____ ones

c) 8 thousands + 15 hundreds + 3 tens + 0 ones = _____

_____

7. Exchange thousands for ten thousands, hundreds for thousands, tens for hundreds, or ones for tens.

a) 2 thousands + 13 hundreds + 2 tens + 5 ones = ____ thousands + ____ hundreds + ____ tens + ____ ones

b) 5 thousands + 2 hundreds + 3 tens + 56 ones = _____

_____

c) 3 ten thousands + 27 thousands + 2 hundreds + 37 tens + 8 ones = _____

_____

 8. Teresa wants to build a model of 6 thousand, 5 hundred and ninety.
She has 5 thousands blocks, 14 hundreds blocks and 30 tens blocks.

Can she build the model?

Use diagrams and numbers to explain your answer.

1. Add the numbers below by drawing a picture and by adding the digits. Use base ten materials to show how to combine the numbers and how to regroup. (The first one has been done for you.)

a) **26 + 36**

	with base ten materials		with numerals	
	tens	ones	tens	ones
26	▮▮	☐☐☐☐☐ ☐	2	6
36	▮▮▮	☐☐☐☐☐ ☐	3	6
sum	▮▮▮▮▮	(☐☐☐☐☐ ☐☐☐☐☐ ☐☐) regroup 10 ones as ten	5	12
	▮▮▮▮▮▮ after regrouping	☐☐	6	2

b) **57 + 27**

	with base ten materials		with numerals	
	tens	ones	tens	ones

2. Add the ones digits. Show how you would regroup 10 ones as 1 ten. The first question has been done for you.

tens go here

a)
```
  [1]
   1 6
 + 1 7
  [3]
```
ones go here

b)
```
  [ ]
   2 4
 + 3 6
   [ ]
```

c)
```
  [ ]
   5 7
 + 1 9
   [ ]
```

d)
```
  [ ]
   7 3
 + 1 9
   [ ]
```

e)
```
  [ ]
   5 7
 + 3 5
   [ ]
```

3. Add the numbers by regrouping. The first one has been done for you.

a)
```
  1
  4 6
+ 2 5
  7 1
```

b)
```
  3 3
+ 4 8
```

c)
```
  7 2
+ 1 9
```

d)
```
  8 5
+ 1 7
```

e)
```
  4 7
+ 2 6
```

f)
```
  3 8
+ 4 3
```

g)
```
  6 9
+   9
```

h)
```
  7 4
+ 1 9
```

i)
```
  4 3
+ 3 9
```

j)
```
  6 8
+ 2 9
```

NS6-11: Adding 3-Digit Numbers

Simon adds **363 + 274** using base ten materials.

363 = 3 hundreds + 6 tens + 3 ones

+ 274 = 2 hundreds + 7 tens + 4 ones

——————————————————————————————

= 5 hundreds + 13 tens + 7 ones

Then, to get the final answer, Simon regroups 10 tens as 1 hundred.

= 6 hundreds + 3 tens + 7 ones

- -

1. Add the numbers below, either by using base ten materials or by drawing a picture in your notebook. Record your work here.

   483 = _____ hundreds + _____ tens + _____ ones

   + 245 = _____ hundreds + _____ tens + _____ ones

   —————————————————————————

   = _____ hundreds + _____ tens + _____ ones

   after regrouping = _____ hundreds + _____ tens + _____ ones

2. Add. You will need to regroup. The first one is started for you.

   a)
   ```
     1
     3 6 4
   + 2 5 3
   ———————
       1 7
   ```
   b)
   ```
     5 7 1
   + 2 5 5
   ```
   c)
   ```
     6 5 2
   +   9 4
   ```
   d)
   ```
     3 6 4
   + 4 8 2
   ```
   e)
   ```
     4 4 7
   + 1 7 2
   ```

3. Add, regrouping where necessary.

   a)
   ```
     1 6 8
   + 3 2 3
   ```
   b)
   ```
     2 5 5
   + 3 6 2
   ```
   c)
   ```
     2 9 5
   + 1 2 3
   ```
   d)
   ```
     4 6 5
   + 1 5 9
   ```
   e)
   ```
     4 5 7
   + 3 0 3
   ```
   f)
   ```
     4 6 5
   + 2 6 4
   ```

4. Add by lining the numbers up correctly in the grid. The first one has been started for you.

   a) 449 + 346   b) 273 + 456   c) 832 + 109   d) 347 + 72

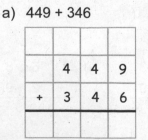
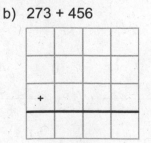
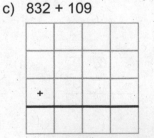
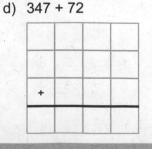

Number Sense 1

Samuel adds **2 974 + 2 313** using base ten materials.

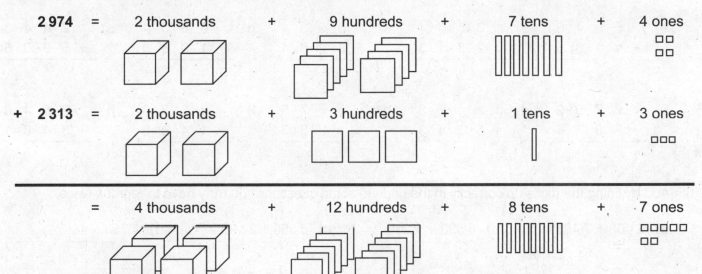

2 974 = 2 thousands + 9 hundreds + 7 tens + 4 ones

+ 2 313 = 2 thousands + 3 hundreds + 1 tens + 3 ones

= 4 thousands + 12 hundreds + 8 tens + 7 ones

Then, to get the final answer, Samuel exchanges 10 hundreds for 1 thousand.

= 5 thousands + 2 hundreds + 8 tens + 7 ones

---

1. Add the numbers below, either by using base ten materials or by drawing a picture in your notebook. Record your work here.

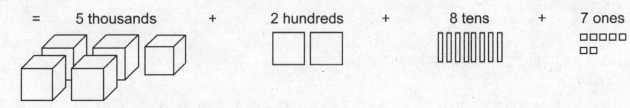

5 486	=	____ thousands + ____ hundreds + ____ tens + ____ ones
+ 3 713	=	____ thousands + ____ hundreds + ____ tens + ____ ones
	=	____ thousands + ____ hundreds + ____ tens + ____ ones
after regrouping	=	____ thousands + ____ hundreds + ____ tens + ____ ones

2. Add. (You will need to regroup.) The first one is started for you.

a)
```
    4 6 8 3
  + 2 7 1 2
  _____
      3 9 5
```

b)
```
    2 5 3 7
  + 4 6 2 1
  _____
```

c)
```
    8 6 5 4
  +   7 2 4
  _____
```

d)
```
    3 1 7 4
  + 4 9 2 3
  _____
```

e)
```
    5 9 4 6
  + 2 4 3 2
  _____
```

3. Add. You will need to regroup tens as hundreds.

a)
```
    8 5 6 3
  + 1 3 5 1
  _____
```

b)
```
    4 4 8 7
  + 2 3 5 1
  _____
```

c)
```
    3 6 8 3
  + 3 1 3 2
  _____
```

d)
```
    2 4 7 8
  +   2 7 1
  _____
```

e)
```
    9 5 9 3
  +   2 5 2
  _____
```

4. Add the following, regrouping or carrying where necessary.

a)   5 8 4 6
   + 1 1 3 5

b)   3 5 6 4
   + 2 8 1 3

c)   6 5 3 4
   + 3 2 9 4

d)   8 8 5 4
   + 1 0 6 3

e)   2 4 4 3
   + 5 9 3 5

f)   6 7 5 2
   + 2 3 3 4

g)   3 4 7 3
   + 5 2 4 3

h)   5 6 7 5
   +   9 2 3

i)   8 2 3 0
   + 1 4 8 8

j)   2 5 4 8
   + 3 4 8 1

5. Add by lining the digits up correctly in the grid. In some questions you may have to regroup twice.

a) 2 468 + 7 431

b) 8 596 + 1 235

c) 6 650 + 2 198

d) 8 359 + 48

6. Add, regrouping where necessary.

a)   5 4 5 5
   + 1 2 7 3

b)   7 3 2 4 6
   + 1 8 3 8 2

c)   1 4 5 6 8 3
   + 3 2 9 2 3 4

d)   2 3 5 2 7 5
   + 5 1 2 9 1 3

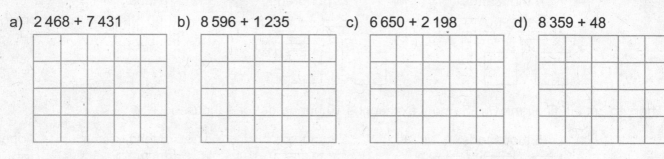

e)   5 326 + 1 234 + 6 762   f)   3 658 + 6 343 + 4 534   g)   389 + 3247 + 712 + 52

7. A **palindrome** is a number (or word) that reads the same forward and backward.

   For instance: 363,   51 815   and   2 375 732   are all palindromes.

   For each number below, follow the steps shown here for the number 124.

   Step 1:   Reverse the digits.   124 → 421

   Step 2:   Add the two numbers.   124 + 421 = 545

   Step 3:   If the number you create is *not* a palindrome repeat Steps 1 and 2 with the new number.
              Most numbers will eventually become palindromes if you keep repeating these steps.

   Create palindromes from the following numbers.

   a) 216   b) 154   c) 651   d) 23153   e) 371   f) 258   g) 1385

NS6-13: Subtraction

Mark subtracts **54 − 17** using base ten materials.

Step 1:
Mark represents 54 with base ten materials…

tens	ones
5	4

Here is how Mark uses numerals to show his work:

```
  54
- 17
```

Step 2:
7 (the ones digit of 17) is greater than 4 (the ones digit of 54) so Mark regroups a tens block as 10 ones…

tens	ones
4	14

Here is how Mark shows the regrouping:

```
  4 14
  5̶ 4̶
- 1 7
```

Step 3:
Mark subtracts 17 (he takes away 1 tens block and 7 ones)…

tens	ones
3	7

And now Mark can subtract 14 − 7 ones and 4 − 1 tens:

```
  4 14
  5̶ 4̶
- 1 7
  3 7
```

---

1. In these questions, Mark doesn't have enough ones to subtract. Help him by regrouping a tens block as 10 ones. Show how he would rewrite his subtraction statement.

a) 53 − 36

tens	ones
5	3

tens	ones
4	13

```
    5 3
  - 3 6
```

```
    4 13
    5̶ 3̶
  - 3 6
```

b) 65 − 29

tens	ones
6	5

tens	ones

```
    6 5
  - 2 9
```

```
    6 5
  - 2 9
```

c) 45 − 27

tens	ones
4	5

tens	ones

```
    4 5
  - 2 7
```

```
    4 5
  - 2 7
```

d) 53 − 48

tens	ones
5	3

tens	ones

```
    5 3
  - 4 8
```

```
    5 3
  - 4 8
```

2. Subtract by regrouping. The first one is done for you.

a)
	7	12
	8̸	2̸
−	3	7
	4	5

b)
	5	4
−	2	6

c)
	7	5
−	3	8

d)
	4	1
−	2	3

e)
	6	7
−	4	9

3. For the questions where you need to regroup, write "Help!" in the space provided.

How do you know when you need to regroup? Write an answer in your notebook. If you are working with a partner, discuss.

a) 58
 − 19   Help!
          8 is less than 9

b) 34
 − 13   _____

c) 85
 − 27   _____

d) 48
 − 42   _____

e) 68
 − 35   _____

f) 91
 − 25   _____

g) 85
 − 24   _____

h) 66
 − 8   _____

i) 25
 − 16   _____

j) 93
 − 47   _____

k) 56
 − 9   _____

l) 85
 − 12   _____

4. To subtract 425 −182, Rita regroups a hundreds block for 10 tens blocks.

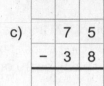

hundreds	tens	ones
4	2	5

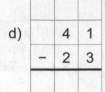

hundreds	tens	ones
3	12	5

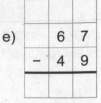

hundreds	tens	ones
2	4	3

Subtract by regrouping <u>hundreds</u> as tens. The first one has been started for you.

a)
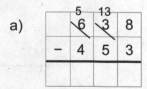

	5	13	
	6̸	3̸	8
−	4	5	3

b)
	8	5	4
−	3	7	2

c)

	7	5	5
−	3	8	2

d)

	4	2	3
−	1	8	2

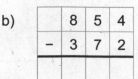

5. Subtract by regrouping <u>tens</u> as ones. The first one has been started for you.

a)

	7		
−	2	4	8

b)

	3	4	3
−	2	1	9

c)

	8	2	5
−	5	1	7

d)

	6	7	1
−	3	1	6

6. For the questions below, you will have to regroup *twice*.

Example: Step 1:   Step 2:   Step 3:   Step 4:   Step 5:

Step 1:
```
   2 16
 8 3 6
- 3 5 8
```

Step 2:
```
   2 16
 8 3 6
- 3 5 8
      8
```

Step 3:
```
      12
   7 2 16
 8 3 6
- 3 5 8
      8
```

Step 4:
```
      12
   7 2 16
 8 3 6
- 3 5 8
    7 8
```

Step 5:
```
      12
   7 2 16
 8 3 6
- 3 5 8
  4 7 8
```

a)

	9	3	4
−	4	5	6

b)

	7	4	7
−	2	6	9

c)

	5	3	2
−		5	9

d)

	8	9	2
−	4	9	5

7. To subtract 5 267 − 3 415, Laura regroups a thousands block as 10 hundreds blocks.

thousands	hundreds	tens	ones
5	2	6	7

thousands	hundreds	tens	ones
4	12	6	7

thousands	hundreds	tens	ones
1	8	5	2

Subtract by regrouping thousands as hundreds. The first one has been done for you.

a)
```
   3 13
 4 3 5 8
- 1 5 2 6
  2 8 3 2
```

b)

	6	5	3	5
−	3	8	1	4

c)

	7	3	6	2
−	4	5	1	2

d)

	9	0	6	3
−	2	7	0	2

8. In some of the questions below, you will need to regroup.

a)

		3	6	4	8
−		1	9	3	4

b)

		9	1	2	4
−		6	0	6	2

c)

		8	5	4	2
−		3	4	6	1

d)

	3	2	8	3	9
−		4	6	2	8

9. In the questions below, you will have to regroup *three* times (i.e. regroup a ten as 10 ones, a hundred as 10 tens and a thousand as 10 hundreds).

Example:

Step 1:

```
  1 13
6 4 2 3
- 3 7 4 6
```

Step 2:

```
  1 13
6 4 2 3
- 3 7 4 6
        7
```

Step 3:

```
   11
3  13
6 4 2 3
- 3 7 4 6
      7 7
```

Step 4:

```
   11
3  13
6 4 2 3
- 3 7 4 6
    6 7 7
```

Step 5:

```
   13 11
5 3  13
6 4 2 3
- 3 7 4 6
  2 6 7 7
```

a)

		9	5	4	2
−		1	7	6	3

b)

		6	4	3	7
−		2	6	7	8

c)

		4	5	6	3
−		1	7	9	5

d)

		7	8	4	3
−		4	8	6	5

10. In the questions below, you will have to regroup *two*, *three* or *four* times.

Example:

Step 1:

```
0 10
1 0 0 0
-   7 5 6
```

Step 2:

```
      9
0 10 10
1 0 0 0
-   7 5 6
```

Step 3:

```
    9 9
0 10 10 10
1 0 0 0
-   7 5 6
```

Step 4:

```
    9 9
0 10 10 10
1 0 0 0
-   7 5 6
    2 4 4
```

a)

	1	0	0	0
−		4	6	8

b)

	1	0	0
−		3	2

c)

1	0	0	0	0
−	6	4	8	6

d)

1	0	0	0	0
−		5	1	1	1

TEACHER:
See the Teacher's Guide for a fast method of subtraction for questions like 10a to d above.

Answer the following questions in your notebook.

1. A school has 150 students.
    80 of the students are boys.

    How many are girls?

2. Raj has 150 stamps.
    Sharif has 12 fewer stamps than Raj.
    Cedric has 15 more stamps than Raj.

    How many stamps do the children have altogether?

3. Camile cycled 2 357 km one year
    and 5 753 km the next.

    How many km did she
    cycle altogether?

4. Two nearby towns have populations
    of 442 670 and 564 839 people.

    What is the total population of both towns?

5. A grocery store had 480 cans of soup.

    In one week they sold:

    *   212 cans of tomato soup
    *   57 cans of chicken soup
    *   43 cans of mushroom soup

    How many cans were left?

6. A box turtle can live 100 years.
    A rabbit can live 15 years.

    How much longer than a rabbit can a box
    turtle live?

7. In the number 432...

    *   The 100s digit is one more than the tens digit
    *   The 10s digit is one more than the ones digit

    Make up your own number with this property.

    _____ _____ _____

    Now write the number backwards.

    _____ _____ _____

    Next write these two numbers in a grid and
    subtract them (be sure to put the greater number
    on top).

    Try this again with several other numbers. You
    will always get 198!

    BONUS
    Can you explain why this works?

8. The shoreline of Lake Ontario is 1 146 km.

    The shoreline of Lake Erie is 1 402 km.

    How much longer is the shoreline of Lake Erie
    than the shoreline of Lake Ontario?

9. The Nile River is about 6 690 km long and
    the Amazon River is 6 440 km long.

    How much longer is the Nile River than the
    Amazon River?

Answer the questions below in your notebook.

1. The chart below gives the area of some of the largest islands in Canada.

Island	Area in km²
Baffin Island	507 450
Ellesmere Island	196 240
Newfoundland	108 860
Vancouver Island	31 290

a) Write the area of the islands in order from least to greatest.

b) How much greater than the area of the smallest island is the area of the largest island?

c) How much greater is the area of Ellesmere Island than Newfoundland?

d) The area of Greenland is 2 166 086 km².

Do Baffin Island and Vancouver Island *together* have an area greater than Greenland?

2. Use each of the digits 4, 5, 6, 7, 8 once to create…

a) the greatest odd number possible.

b) a number between 56 700 and 57 000.

c) an even number whose tens digit and hundreds digit add to 12.

d) a number as close to 70 000 as possible (explain how you know your answer is correct).

3. There are 390 000 species of plants and 1 234 400 species of animals.

How many more species of animals are there than plants?

4. Use the numbers 1, 2, 3, 4 once in each question.

a)

$$
\begin{array}{r}
\square\ \square \\
+\ \ 2\ \square \\
\hline
\square\ \ 6
\end{array}
$$

b)

$$
\begin{array}{r}
\square\ \square \\
-\ \ \square\ \square \\
\hline
1\ \ 1
\end{array}
$$

c)

$$
\begin{array}{r}
\square\ \square \\
+\ \ \square\ \square \\
\hline
5\ \ 5
\end{array}
$$

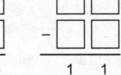

5. Here are some important dates in the history of science.

- In 1543, Copernicus published a book claiming the sun is the center of our solar system.
- In 1610, Galileo Galilei used his newly invented telescope to discover the moons of Jupiter.
- In 1667, Isaac Newton announced his law of gravity.

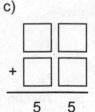

a) How long ago did Copernicus publish his book?

b) How many years passed between each pair of dates given?

When you multiply a pair of numbers, the result is called the **product** of the numbers. You can represent a product using an **array**.

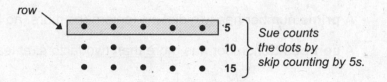

Sue counts the dots by skip counting by 5s.

Sue writes a multiplication statement for the array: **3 × 5 = 15**   (3 and 5 are called **factors** of 15)

----

1. Write a multiplication statement for each array.

a)

_3_ rows

_4_ dots in each row

3 × 4 = 12

b)

____ rows

____ dots in each row

_____

c)

_____

_____

_____

2. Write a product for each array.

a)

4 × 3

rows   dots in each row

b)

_____

c)

_____

d)

_____

3. Draw arrays for these products.

a) 2 × 5   b) 3 × 7   c) 4 × 6   d) 1 × 8   e) 4 × 2

4. There are only *three* ways to arrange 4 dots in an array.
   So there are only 3 ways to write 4 as a product of two factors.

   • • • •   1 × 4 = 4   2 × 2 = 4   4 × 1 = 4

   How many ways can you write each number as a product of two factors? (Draw arrays to help.)

   a) 6   b) 8   c) 9   d) 10   e) 12

5. The numbers that appear beside the arrays in Question 4 are called the **factors** of 4.
   The factors of 4 are the numbers 1, 2, and 4.

   Write a list of factors for the numbers 6, 8, 9, 10, and 12.

A **prime** number has <u>two</u> distinct factors (no more, no less): itself and 1.

A **composite** number has <u>more than two</u> factors: at least one number **other than** itself and 1.

----

1. a) How many <u>distinct</u> factors does the number 1 have? _____   b) Is 1 a prime number? _____

2. List all the prime numbers less than 10: _____

3. List all the composite numbers between 10 and 20: _____

4. What is the greatest prime number less than 30? _____

5. Circle the prime numbers.

    1   25   14   13   17   20   27   15   12   18   29   33

6. Eratosthenes was a Libyan scholar who lived over 2000 years ago.
    He developed a method to systematically identify prime numbers.
    It is called **Eratosthenes' Sieve**.

    Follow the directions below to identify the prime numbers from 1 to 100.

    a) Cross out the number 1 (it is not prime).

    b) Circle 2, and cross out all the multiples of 2.

    c) Circle 3, and cross out all the multiples of 3
        (that haven't already been crossed out).

    d) Circle 5, and cross out all the multiples of 5
        (that haven't already been crossed out).

    e) Circle 7, and cross out all the multiples of 7
        (that haven't already been crossed out).

    f) Circle all remaining numbers.

    You've just used **Eratosthenes' Sieve** to find
    all the prime numbers from 1 to100!

1	2	3	4	5	6	7	8	9	10
11	12	13	14	15	16	17	18	19	20
21	22	23	24	25	26	27	28	29	30
31	32	33	34	35	36	37	38	39	40
41	42	43	44	45	46	47	48	49	50
51	52	53	54	55	56	57	58	59	60
61	62	63	64	65	66	67	68	69	70
71	72	73	74	75	76	77	78	79	80
81	82	83	84	85	86	87	88	89	90
91	92	93	94	95	96	97	98	99	100

7. The prime numbers 3 and 5 differ by 2.
    Find three pairs of prime numbers less than 20 that differ by 2.

1. List all the factors of each number (the first one is done for you).

   a) 25: _____1, 5, 25_____   b) 8: _____

   c) 12: _____   d) 16: _____

   e) 9: _____   f) 18: _____

   g) 50: _____   h) 45: _____

   i) 60: _____   j) 42: _____

2. Put a check mark In front of the numbers that are composite numbers.

   ____ 30   ____ 31   ____ 32   ____ 33   ____ 34   ____ 35   ____ 36   ____ 37

3. Write a number between 0 and 20 that has …

   a) two factors: _____   b) four factors: _____   c) five factors _____

4. Cross out any number that is *not* a multiple of 4. | 12   19   34   20   50   40 |

5. Write the three numbers less than 40 that have 2 and 5 as factors: _____ _____ _____

ADVANCED
6. Write three consecutive composite numbers.   ☐ ☐ ☐

7. Write five odd multiples of 3 between 10 and 40: _____ _____ _____ _____ _____

8. I am a prime number less than 10.
   If you add 10 or 20 to me, the result is a prime number.
   What number am I?

9. Which number is neither prime nor composite? Explain.

10. Find the **sum** of the first five composite numbers. Show your work.

11. How many prime numbers are there between 30 and 50? Explain how you know.

Any composite number can be written as a product of prime numbers.
This product is called the **prime factorization** of the original number.

Example: Find a prime factorization of 20.

It can't be 10 × 2 (because the number 10 is a composite number).

5 × 2 × 2 is a prime factorization of 20.

----

1. You can find a prime factorization for a number by using a **factor tree**. Here is how you can make a factor tree for the number 20.

Step 1:
Find any pair of numbers (not including one) that multiply to give 20.

Step 2:
Repeat Step 1 for the numbers on the "branches" of the tree.

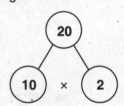

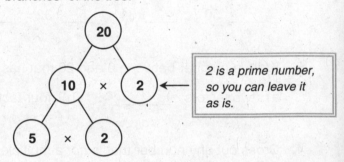

2 is a prime number, so you can leave it as is.

Complete the factor tree for the numbers below.

a)

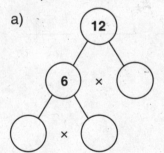

b)

c)

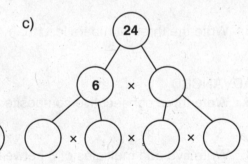

2. Write a prime factorization for each number below. The first one is started for you.
   HINT: It helps to first find any factorization and then factor any composite numbers in the factorization.

   a) 30 = 10 × 3 =   b) 18 =

   c) 8 =   d) 14 =

 3. Using a factor tree, find prime factorizations for:

   a) 30   b) 36   c) 27   d) 28   e) 75

4. Here are some branching patterns for factor trees.

   Can you find a factor tree for the number 24 that looks different from the tree in Question 1 c)?

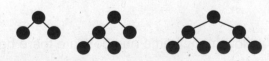

To multiply **4 × 20**, Allen makes 4 groups containing 2 <u>tens</u> blocks (20 = 2 tens).

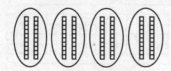

$$4 \times 20 = 4 \times 2 \text{ tens}$$
$$= 8 \text{ tens}$$
$$= 80$$

To multiply **4 × 200**, Allen makes 4 groups containing 2 <u>hundreds</u> blocks (200 = 2 hundreds).

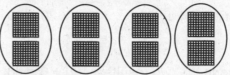

$$4 \times 200 = 4 \times 2 \text{ hundreds}$$
$$= 8 \text{ hundreds}$$
$$= 800$$

Allen notices a pattern:

$$4 \times 2 \quad = 8$$
$$4 \times 20 \quad = 80$$
$$4 \times 200 = 800$$

----

1. Draw a model for each multiplication statement, then calculate the answer. The first one is done.

   a) 5 × 30

   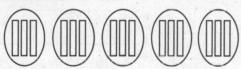

   b) 3 × 40

   5 × 30 = 5 × __3__ tens = __15__ tens = __150__   3 × 40 = 3 × ____ tens = ____ tens = ____

2. Regroup to find the answer.

   a) 3 × 60 = 3 × _____ tens = _____ tens = _____

   b) 6 × 50 = 6 × _____ tens = _____ tens = _____

   c) 4 × 50 = 4 × _____ tens = _____ tens = _____

   d) 5 × 40 = 5 × _____ tens = _____ tens = _____

3. Complete the pattern by multiplying.

   a) 5 × 3 = _____   b) 6 × 1 = _____   c) 3 × 4 = _____   d) 4 × 5 = _____

      5 × 30 = _____   6 × 10 = _____   3 × 40 = _____   4 × 50 = _____

      5 × 300 = _____   6 × 100 = _____   3 × 400 = _____   4 × 500 = _____

4. Multiply.

   a) 7 × 30 = _____   b) 30 × 5 = _____   c) 3 × 40 = _____   d) 80 × 3 = _____

   e) 4 × 400 = _____   f) 500 × 8 = _____   g) 5 × 80 = _____   h) 300 × 6 = _____

   i) 3 × 900 = _____   j) 700 × 6 = _____   k) 8 × 20 = _____   l) 700 × 3 = _____

5. Draw a base ten model (using cubes to represent thousands) to show: 7 × 1 000 = 7 000.

6. Knowing that 6 × 3 = 18, how can you use this fact to multiply 6 × 3 000? Explain.

To multiply **4 × 22**,
Leela rewrites 22 as a sum: $22 = 20 + 2$

She first multiplies 4 by 20: $4 \times 20 = 80$

Next she multiplies 4 by 2: $4 \times 2 = 8$

Finally she adds the two results: $80 + 8 = 88$

So Leela can conclude that **4 × 22 = 88**:

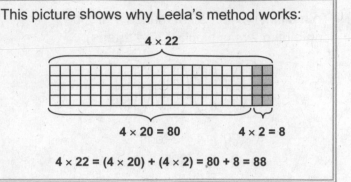

This picture shows why Leela's method works:

$$4 \times 22 = (4 \times 20) + (4 \times 2) = 80 + 8 = 88$$

---

1. Use the picture to write the multiplication statement as a sum. The first one is started for you.

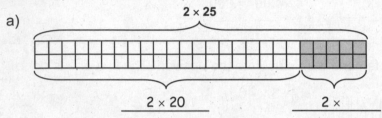

   a) **2 × 25**

   $\underline{\quad 2 \times 20 \quad}$ $\underline{\quad 2 \times \quad}$

   $2 \times 25 = (2 \times \underline{\quad}) + (2 \times \underline{\quad})$

   b) **3 × 15**

   $\underline{\qquad}$ $\underline{\qquad}$

   $3 \times 15 = (\underline{\qquad}) + (\underline{\qquad})$

2. Multiply using Leela's method. The first one has been done for you.

   a) $5 \times 13 = \underline{\quad 5 \times 10 \quad} + \underline{\quad 5 \times 3 \quad} = \underline{\quad 50 + 15 \quad} = \underline{\quad 65 \quad}$

   b) $4 \times 21 = \underline{\qquad} + \underline{\qquad} = \underline{\qquad} = \underline{\qquad}$

   c) $3 \times 43 = \underline{\qquad} + \underline{\qquad} = \underline{\qquad} = \underline{\qquad}$

   d) $2 \times 432 = \underline{\quad 2 \times 400 \quad} + \underline{\quad 2 \times 30 \quad} + \underline{\quad 2 \times 2 \quad} = \underline{\quad 800 + 60 + 4 \quad} = \underline{\quad 864 \quad}$

   e) $3 \times 312 = \underline{\qquad\qquad\qquad\qquad\qquad}$

   f) $4 \times 321 = \underline{\qquad\qquad\qquad\qquad\qquad}$

3. Multiply in your head by multiplying the digits separately.

   a) $3 \times 12 = \underline{\qquad}$
   b) $3 \times 52 = \underline{\qquad}$
   c) $6 \times 31 = \underline{\qquad}$
   d) $7 \times 21 = \underline{\qquad}$

   e) $5 \times 31 = \underline{\qquad}$
   f) $3 \times 43 = \underline{\qquad}$
   g) $6 \times 51 = \underline{\qquad}$
   h) $2 \times 44 = \underline{\qquad}$

   i) $4 \times 521 = \underline{\qquad}$
   j) $3 \times 621 = \underline{\qquad}$
   k) $5 \times 411 = \underline{\qquad}$
   l) $2 \times 444 = \underline{\qquad}$

   m) $3 \times 632 = \underline{\qquad}$
   n) $4 \times 422 = \underline{\qquad}$
   o) $4 \times 212 = \underline{\qquad}$
   p) $2 \times 421 = \underline{\qquad}$

4. a) Stacy placed 821 books in each of 4 bookshelves.
      How many books did she place altogether?

   b) Nickalo put 723 pencils in each of 3 boxes.
      How many pencils did he put in the boxes?

Number Sense 1

Clara uses a chart to multiply 3 × 42:

Step 1:
She multiplies the ones digit of 42 by 3 (3 × 2 = 6).

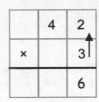

Step 2:
She multiplies the tens digit of 42 by 3 (3 × 4 tens = 12 tens).

She regroups 10 tens as 1 hundred.

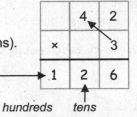

hundreds   tens

1. Use Clara's method to find the products.

a)   5 1
   ×   3

b)   8 2
   ×   3

c)   6 2
   ×   2

d)   5 1
   ×   4

e)   5 1
   ×   5

f)   6 1
   ×   6

g)   8 3
   ×   3

h)   7 4
   ×   2

i)   9 4
   ×   2

j)   4 2
   ×   4

k)   8 3
   ×   2

l)   4 1
   ×   5

m)   3 1
   ×   7

n)   3 2
   ×   4

o)   6 3
   ×   2

p)   6 3
   ×   3

q)   2 2
   ×   4

r)   3 1
   ×   9

s)   4 1
   ×   5

t)   6 1
   ×   9

u)   8 1
   ×   7

v)   9 2
   ×   3

w)   9 2
   ×   4

x)   5 2
   ×   3

y)   5 2
   ×   4

z)   8 3
   ×   4

aa)   9 3
    ×   2

bb)   7 1
    ×   9

cc)   5 3
    ×   3

dd)   6 2
    ×   3

ee)   4 4
    ×   2

ff)   6 4
    ×   2

gg)   5 1
    ×   5

hh)   8 1
    ×   7

ii)   9 3
    ×   3

2. Find the following products.

a) 3 × 63   b) 6 × 50   c) 5 × 61   d) 2 × 94   e) 4 × 42

Alicia uses a chart to multiply 3 × 24:

<u>Step 1:</u>
She multiples 4 ones by 3 (4 × 3 = 12).

She regroups 10 ones as 1 ten.

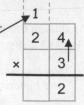

<u>Step 2:</u>
She multiples 2 tens by 3 (3 × 2 tens = 6 tens).

She adds 1 ten to the result (6 + 1 = 7 tens).

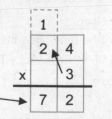

1. Using Alicia's method, complete the <u>first</u> step of the multiplication. The first one has been done.

a)
```
    1
  1   2
×     6
─────────
      2
```

b)
```
  2   5
×     3
─────────
```

c)
```
  2   5
×     4
─────────
```

d)
```
  1   6
×     6
─────────
```

e)
```
  4   9
×     2
─────────
```

2. Using Alicia's method, complete the <u>second</u> step of multiplication.

a)

```
    1
  2   4
×     4
─────────
  9   6
```

b)
```
    1
  3   5
×     3
─────────
      5
```

c)
```
    2
  1   5
×     5
─────────
      5
```

d)
```
    1
  1   3
×     6
─────────
      8
```

e)
```
    2
  1   6
×     4
─────────
      4
```

f)
```
    1
  4   6
×     2
─────────
      2
```

g)
```
    2
  4   8
×     3
─────────
      4
```

h)
```
    1
  2   5
×     3
─────────
      5
```

i)
```
    2
  2   9
×     3
─────────
      7
```

j)
```
    3
  1   6
×     6
─────────
      6
```

3. Using Alicia's method, complete the <u>first</u> and <u>second</u> steps of the multiplication.

a)
```
  3   5
×     2
─────────
```

b)
```
  1   5
×     6
─────────
```

c)
```
  1   8
×     5
─────────
```

d)
```
  2   5
×     3
─────────
```

e)
```
  2   4
×     4
─────────
```

f)
```
  2   7
×     5
─────────
```

g)
```
  3   2
×     8
─────────
```

h)
```
  3   5
×     6
─────────
```

i)
```
  2   6
×     7
─────────
```

j)
```
  4   6
×     8
─────────
```

Dillon multiplies **2 × 213** in <u>three</u> different ways.

1. With a chart:

	hundreds	tens	ones
	2	1	3
×			2
	4	2	6

2. In expanded form:

$$200 + 10 + 3$$
$$\times\ 2$$
$$= 400 + 20 + 6$$
$$= 426$$

3. With base ten materials:

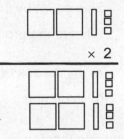

---

1. Rewrite the multiplication statement in expanded notation. Then perform the multiplication.

a)　234　　＿＿＿ + ＿＿＿ + ＿＿＿
　　× 2　　　　　　　　　　　　× 2
　　　　　　= ＿＿ + ＿＿ + ＿＿
　　　　　　= ＿＿

b)　133　　＿＿＿ + ＿＿＿ + ＿＿＿
　　× 3　　　　　　　　　　　　× 3
　　　　　　= ＿＿ + ＿＿ + ＿＿
　　　　　　= ＿＿

2. Multiply.

a)
	4	1
×		4

b)
4	3	4
×		2

c)
3	1	2
×		3

d)
1	2	4
×		2

e)
3	2	3
×		3

3. Multiply by regrouping ones as tens.

a)
2	2	7
×		2

b)
2	1	6
×		4

c)
2	2	4
×		3

d)
4	3	6
×		2

e)
1	1	6
×		6

4. Multiply by regrouping tens as hundreds. In the last question, you will also regroup ones as tens.

a)
3	6	4
×		2

b)
1	5	1
×		6

c)
2	4	2
×		4

d)
1	7	1
×		5

e)
2	5	6
×		3

 5. Multiply.

　　a) 5 × 134　　b) 7 × 421　　c) 6 × 132　　d) 9 × 134　　e) 8 × 124　　f) 6 × 135

6. Draw a picture in your notebook to show the result of the multiplication.

a)
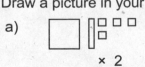
× 2

b)
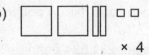
× 4

c)
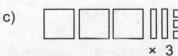
× 3

1. a)   Skip count by 10 fifteen times. What number did you reach? _____

    b)   What is the product: 10 × 15 = _____

    c)   Skip count by 100 fifteen times. What number did you reach? _____

    d)   What is the product: 100 × 15 = _____

2. How many zeroes do you add to a number when you multiply the number by…

    a) 10? You add ___ zero.   b) 100? You add ____ zeroes.   c) 1000? You add ____ zeroes.

3. Continue the pattern.

    a)   10 × 6 = _____   b)   10 × 36 = _____   c)   10 × 85 = _____

          100 × 6 = _____   100 × 36 = _____   100 × 85 = _____

          1000 × 6 = _____   1000 × 36 = _____   1000 × 85 = _____

          10 000 × 6 = _____   10 000 × 36 = _____   10 000 × 85 = _____

4. Find the products.

    a) 19 × 10 = _____   b) 10 × 56 = _____   c) 10 × 83 = _____

    d) 42 × 100 = _____   e) 80 × 100 = _____   f) 13 × 100 = _____

    g) 100 × 40 = _____   h) 10 × 23 = _____   i) 1 000 × 6 = _____

    j) 572 × 10 = _____   k) 1 000 × 28 = _____   l) 93 × 1 000 = _____

5. Round each number to the **leading digit**.

    Then find the product of the rounded numbers.

    > The first (non-zero) digit in a number
    > – that is, the furthest to the left –
    > is called the **leading digit**.

    leading digit

    a) 12 × 29   b) 11 × 23   c) 12 × 58   d) 13 × 74   e) 68 × 110   f) 61 × 120

10 × 30
= 300

6. Al works 38 hours a week. He earns $12 per hour.
    About how much is his weekly income?
    How did you find your answer?

7. How many hundred dollar bills would you need to make …

    a) one hundred thousand dollars?   b) one million dollars? Explain.

8. Which amount is worth more: 25 723 dimes or 231 524 pennies?

Erin wants to multiply **20 × 32**.

She knows how to find 10 × 32, so she rewrites 20 × 32 as <u>double</u> 10 × 32.

$$20 × 32 = 2 × \mathbf{10 × 32}$$
$$= 2 × 320$$
$$= 640$$

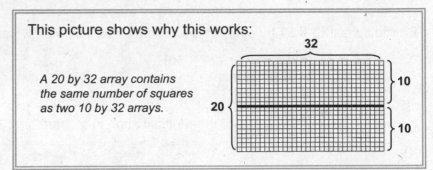

This picture shows why this works:

A 20 by 32 array contains the same number of squares as two 10 by 32 arrays.

---

1. Write each number as a product of two factors (where one of the factors is 10).

   a) 30 = <u>3 × 10</u>   b) 40 = _____   c) 70 = _____   d) 50 = _____

2. Write an equivalent product for each array. The first one is done for you.

   a)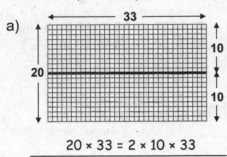

   20 × 33 = 2 × 10 × 33

   b)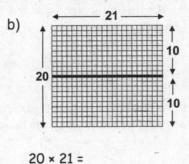

   20 × 21 =

   c)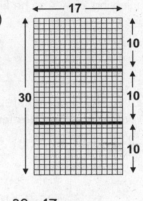

   30 × 17 =

3. Find each product in two stages.

   <u>Step 1</u>: Multiply the second number by 10
   <u>Step 2</u>: Multiply the result by the tens digit of the first number

   a) 20 × 24 = <u>2 × 240</u>   b) 30 × 32 = _____   c) 40 × 12 = _____   d) 50 × 41 = _____
       = _____   = _____   = _____   = _____

4. Find each product mentally.

   a) 30 × 33 = _____   b) 20 × 60 = _____   c) 20 × 80 = _____   d) 40 × 34 = _____

   e) 20 × 42 = _____   f) 30 × 83 = _____   g) 64 × 20 = _____   h) 30 × 74 = _____

   i) 40 × 42 = _____   j) 30 × 53 = _____   k) 60 × 51 = _____   l) 91 × 50 = _____

   m) 60 × 30 = _____   n) 80 × 40 = _____   o) 52 × 90 = _____   p) 18 × 30 = _____

5. Estimate each product. (Round each factor to the leading digit.)

   a) 36 × 58 ≈ <u>40 × 60 = 2 400</u>   b) 33 × 72 ≈ _____   c) 28 × 82 ≈ _____

   d) 63 × 48 ≈ _____   e) 71 × 32 ≈ _____   f) 21 × 16 ≈ _____

Ed multiplies **20 × 37** by splitting the product into a sum of two smaller products.

20 × 37 = (20 × 7) + (20 × 30)
          = 140 + 600
          = 740

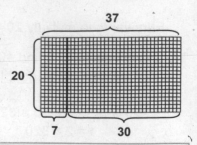

He keeps track of the steps of the multiplication in a chart.

Step 1:
Ed multiplies 2 × 7 = 14. He is really multiplying **20 × 7** so he first writes a zero in the ones place.

Step 2:
Next, since 2 × 7 = 14, Ed writes the 4 in the tens place and the 1 at the top of the hundreds column.

Step 3:
Ed then multiplies **20 × 30** (= 600). As a short cut, he multiplies 2 × 3 = 6 and then he adds the 1 from the top of the hundreds column: 6 + 1 = 7 (= 700).

----

1. Practice the first two steps of the multiplication (given above). The first one is done for you.
   NOTE: In one of the questions you will not need to regroup the hundreds.

   a) b) c) d) e)

2. Multiply.

   a)  b)  c)  d) 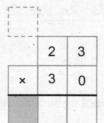 e)

   f)
   $$\begin{array}{r} 3\ 6 \\ \times\ 3\ 0 \\ \hline \end{array}$$
   g)
   $$\begin{array}{r} 4\ 2 \\ \times\ 2\ 0 \\ \hline \end{array}$$
   h)
   $$\begin{array}{r} 2\ 6 \\ \times\ 4\ 0 \\ \hline \end{array}$$
   i)
   $$\begin{array}{r} 1\ 2 \\ \times\ 6\ 0 \\ \hline \end{array}$$
   j)
   $$\begin{array}{r} 3\ 2 \\ \times\ 7\ 0 \\ \hline \end{array}$$

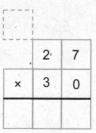 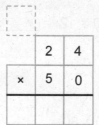 

3. Rewrite each product as a sum then find the answer.

   a)   20 × 14 =   (20 × 10) + (20 × 4) = 200 + 80 = 280

   b)   30 × 23 = _____

   c)   40 × 32 = _____

NS6-28: Multiplying – 2-Digit by 2-Digit

Grace multiplies **26 × 28** by splitting the product into a sum of two smaller products.

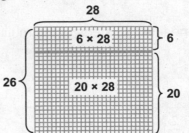

$$26 \times 28 = (6 \times 28) + (20 \times 28)$$
$$= 168 + 560$$
$$= 728$$

She keeps track of the steps of the multiplication using a chart.

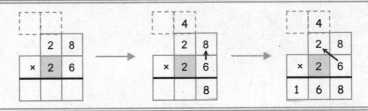

Step 1:
She multiplies **6 × 28**:

1. Practice the first step of the multiplication.

a)

	2	4
×	1	3

b)

	3	6
×	2	3

c)

	3	3
×	3	6

d)

	6	2
×	4	4

e)

	1	6
×	3	5

f)

	2	5
×	4	3

g)

	3	6
×	4	3

h)

	2	4
×	5	6

i)

	3	4
×	2	6

j)

	3	7
×	1	8

Step 2:
Grace multiplies **20 × 28**.
(Notice that she starts by writing a 0 in the ones place because she is multiplying by 20.)

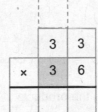

2. Practice the second step of the multiplication.

a)

	3	4
×	4	3
1	0	2

b)

	4	5
×	2	4
1	8	0

c)

	6	9
×	6	2
1	3	8

d)

	5	6
×	3	6
3	3	6

e)

	6	7
×	2	5
3	3	5

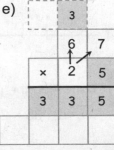

jump math
MULTIPLYING POTENTIAL

Number Sense 1

3. Practice the first two steps of the multiplication.

a)
```
      3   5
  ×   2   6
```

b)
```
      1   3
  ×   3   7
```

c)
```
      3   2
  ×   5   4
```

d)
```
      4   5
  ×   3   5
```

e)
```
      1   6
  ×   4   2
```

f)
```
      4   5
  ×   3   4
```

g)
```
      2   3
  ×   4   5
```

h)
```
      1   8
  ×   2   6
```

i)
```
      9   2
  ×   3   2
```

j)
```
      7   5
  ×   6   3
```

Step 3:
Grace completes the multiplication by adding the products of **6 × 28** and **20 × 28**

---

4. Complete the multiplication by adding the numbers in the last two rows of the chart.

a)
```
    1   4
    2   8
  × 2   6
  ─────────
    1   6   8
+   5   6   0
  ─────────
    7   2   8
```

b)
```
    2   3
    5   4
  × 6   8
  ─────────
    4   3   2
+ 3   2   4   0
```

c)
```
    2   1
    7   6
  × 4   3
  ─────────
    2   2   8
+ 3   0   4   0
```

d)
```
    4   2
    2   7
  × 6   3
  ─────────
    8   1
+ 1   6   2   0
```

e)
```
    4   3
    1   9
  × 5   4
  ─────────
    7   6
+ 9   5   0
```

5. Multiply.

a)
```
      3   4
  ×   4   5
  ─────────

          0
```

b)
```
      1   9
  ×   6   4
```

c)
```
      7   4
  ×   5   2
```

d)
```
      5   4
  ×   3   4
```

e)
```
      8   7
  ×   3   2
```

6. Find the products.

   a) 35 × 23   b) 64 × 81   c) 25 × 43   d) 42 × 87   e) 13 × 94   f) 28 × 37

1. Double the ones and tens separately and add the result: $2 \times 36 = 2 \times 30 + 2 \times 6 = 60 + 12 = 72$.

	25	45	16	28	18	17	35	55	39
Double									

2. The arrays of squares show that $2 \times 3 = 3 \times 2$:

    2×3

    3×2

    a) On grid paper, draw an array of squares to show that $7 \times 5 = 5 \times 7$

    b) If A and B are numbers, is A × B always equal to B × A? Explain.

    c) Draw all the rectangular arrays that you can make using 12 squares.
        How do the arrays show the factors of 12?

3. Rearrange the products so you can find the answer mentally.

    Example: $2 \times 8 \times 35$
    $= 2 \times 35 \times 8$
    $= 70 \times 8$
    $= 560$

    Example: $4 \times 18 \times 25$
    $= 4 \times 25 \times 18$
    $= 100 \times 18$
    $= 1800$

    > **REMEMBER:**
    > $2 \times 250 = 500$
    > $4 \times 250 = 1\,000$

    a) $2 \times 7 \times 25$

    b) $4 \times 84 \times 25$

    c) $2 \times 29 \times 500$

    d) $4 \times 475 \times 25$

    e) $2 \times 36 \times 2 \times 250$

    f) $25 \times 2 \times 50 \times 4$

    g) $2 \times 2 \times 15 \times 250$

    h) $2 \times 853 \times 500$

    i) $4 \times 952 \times 25$

4.

Printer	Printing Rate
A	1 page every 2 seconds
B	90 pages per minute
C	2 pages every second
D	160 pages in 2 minutes

Which printer is the fastest?
Explain how you know.

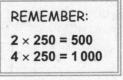

5.

Amount	Cost
First 20	32 cents for each mango
Next 20	25 cents for each mango
More than 40	17 cents for each mango

The chart shows the price a grocery store pays for mangos.
How much would the following amounts cost?

a) 15 mangos

b) 30 mangos

c) 50 mangos

1. You can multiply a 3-digit number by a 2-digit number using the method you learned previously.

   Multiply.

   a)
	3	2	
	2	1	
	3	7	4
	×	5	3
1	1	2	2
1	8	7	0
1	9	8	2	2

   b)
	4	6	9
	×	2	3

   c)
	6	8	5
	×	2	7

2. Cross out any number that is <u>not</u> a multiple of 4.

   13　　24　　32　　50　　40　　2　　27

3. Write the odd multiples of 7 that are between 20 and 80.

   [ ]　[ ]　[ ]　[ ]　[ ]

4. What is the fifth prime number? Explain how you know.

5. Multiply.

   a) 569 × 34　　b) 792 × 87　　c) 926 × 96　　d) 5243 × 88

6. The Karakoran mountain range in Tibet pushes up 2 cm a year.
   How much higher will the range be in 500 years?

7. Each basket holds 47 apples each. There are 326 baskets.
   How many apples are there altogether?

8. What is the largest factor of 24 that is less than 24?

9. Hassim plays basketball every week for 136 minutes.
   He needs 1 350 minutes to get a job at the summer camp.
   If he plays for 7 weeks, will he have enough hours?

10. Find the missing digits.

    a)
	3	[ ]	4
×			3
	9	7	2

    b)
	7	[ ]	7
×			5
3	8	8	5

    c)
	2	5	2
×		[ ]	
1	0	0	8

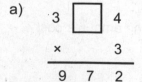
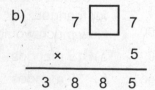
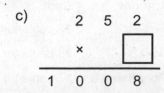

Abdul has 16 apples. A tray holds 4. There are 4 trays.

What has been shared or divided into **sets** or **groups**?   (*Apples.*)

How many **sets** are there?   (*There are 4 sets of apples.*)

How many of the things being divided are in each **set**?   (*There are 4 apples in each set.*)

---

1. a)

What has been shared or divided into sets?

_____

How many sets? *group* **2**

How many in each set? **4**

b)

What has been shared or divided into sets?

_____ **6**

How many sets? **3**

How many in each set? **2**

2.

	What has been shared or divided into sets?	How many sets?	How many in each set?
a) 8 books for each student 32 books 4 students			
b) 4 flowers in each vase 6 flower vases 24 flowers			
c) 5 apples on each tray 20 apples 4 trays			
d) 3 trees in each row 7 rows 21 trees			

3. Using circles for <u>sets</u> and dots for <u>things</u>, draw a picture to show…

a) 6 sets
   3 things in each set

b) 4 groups
   5 things in each group

c) 2 sets
   9 things in each set

Amanda has 16 cookies. There are two ways she can **share** (or divide) her cookies equally.

Method 1:   She can decide how many <u>sets</u> (or <u>groups</u>) of cookies she wants to make.

Example:

Amanda wants to make 4 sets of cookies. She draws 4 circles. ○ ○ ○ ○
She then puts one cookie at a time into the circles until she
has placed all 16 cookies.

Method 2:   She can decide how many cookies she wants to put <u>in each set</u>.

Example:

Amanda wants to put 4 cookies in each set. She counts out 4 cookies.
She keeps counting out sets of 4 cookies until she has placed all
16 cookies into sets.

---

1. Share **24** dots equally. How many dots are in each set?
    HINT: Place one dot at a time.

    a) 4 sets: ○ ○ ○ ○   b) 6 sets: ○ ○ ○ ○ ○ ○

    There are _____ dots in each set.   There are _____ dots in each set.

2. Share the shapes equally among the sets.
    HINT: Count the shapes first. Divide by the number of circles.

    △ △ △ △
    △ △ △ △   a) ○ ○ ○   b) ○ ○ ○ ○
    △ △ △ △

3. Share the squares equally among the sets.

    ☐ ☐ ☐ ☐ ☐ ☐
    ☐ ☐ ☐ ☐ ☐ ☐   ○ ○ ○ ○ ○ ○
    ☐ ☐ ☐ ☐ ☐ ☐

4. Group the lines so that there are three lines in each set. Say how many sets there are.

    a) | | | | | | | | | b) | | | | | | | | | | | | | | | | | | c) | | | | | | | | | |

    There are _____ sets.   There are _____ sets   There are _____ sets.

5. Group **18** candies so that…

    a) there are 9 candies in each set.   b) there are 6 candies in each set.

Number Sense 1

6. In each question, fill in what you know. Write a question mark for what you don't know.

	What has been shared or divided into sets?	How many sets? or How many in each set?
a) Beth has 42 marbles. She puts 6 marbles in each jar.	marbles	There are 6 marbles in each set
b) 30 people in 6 cars.	people	There are 6 sets of people.
c) Jenny has 18 stickers. She gives them to her 2 sisters.		
d) Mike has 40 pictures. He puts 8 in each page of the album.		
e) 24 children are sitting at 3 tables.		
f) 35 flowers are in 5 vases.		

7. Divide the dots into sets.
   HINT: If you know the number of sets, start by drawing circles for sets. If you know the number of things in each set, fill one circle at a time with the correct number of dots.

   a) 21 dots; 3 sets   b) 14 dots; 7 dots in each set

   _____ dots in each set   _____ sets

   c) 36 dots; 9 dots in each set.   d) 20 dots; 4 sets.

You can solve the division problem **12 ÷ 4 = ?** by skip counting on the number line.

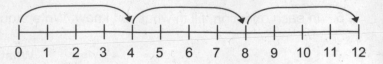

If you divide 12 into sets of size 4, how many sets do you get? The number line shows that it takes three skips of size 4 to get 12.

$$4 + 4 + 4 = 12 \quad so... \quad 12 ÷ 4 = 3$$

- -

1. Use the number line to find the answer to the division statement. Be sure to draw arrows to show your skip counting.

    a)
    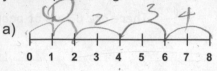

    8 ÷ 2 = __4__

    b)
    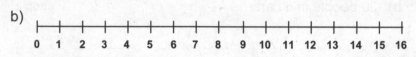

    16 ÷ 8 = __2__

2. What division statement does the picture represent?

    a)
    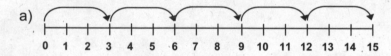

    _____

    b)
    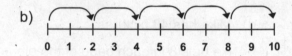

    _____

3. You can also find the answer to a division question by skip counting on your fingers.

    For instance, to find **45 ÷ 9**, count by 9s until you reach 45… the number of fingers you have up when you say "45" is the answer.

    So 45 ÷ 9 = 5

    Find the answers by skip counting on your fingers.

    a) 35 ÷ 5 = __7__   b) 12 ÷ 6 = __2__   c) 32 ÷ 8 = __4__   d) 21 ÷ 7 = __3__   e) 45 ÷ 5 = __9__

    f) 36 ÷ 4 = __9__   g) 25 ÷ 5 = __5__   h) 42 ÷ 6 = __7__   i) 27 ÷ 3 = __9__   j) 16 ÷ 2 = __8__

    k) 36 ÷ 6 = __6__   l) 35 ÷ 7 = __5__   m) 18 ÷ 3 = __6__   n) 21 ÷ 3 = __7__   o) 40 ÷ 8 = __5__

4. 24 flowers are in 6 bouquets. How many flowers in each bouquet? __4__

5. 36 trees are in 9 rows. How many trees are in each row? __4__

6. Amy uses 8 pencils in a month. How many months will she take to use 32 pencils? _____

Win-Chi wants to share 13 pancakes with 3 friends.
He sets out 4 plates, one for himself and one for each of his friends.
He puts one pancake at a time on a plate.

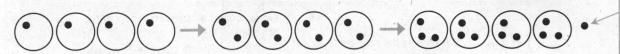

There is one pancake left over.

Thirteen pancakes cannot be shared equally into 4 sets.
Each person gets 3 pancakes, but *one* is left over.
This is the remainder.

13 ÷ 4 = 3 Remainder 1   OR   13 ÷ 4 = 3 R1   NOTE: R means "remainder"

----

1. Can you share 9 pancakes equally onto 2 plates?
   Show your work using dots for pancakes and circles for plates.

2. For each question, share the dots as equally as possible among the circles.

   a) 10 dots in 3 circles

   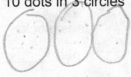

   ___10___ dots in each circle; ___1___ dots remaining

   b) 17 dots in 4 circles

   ___17___ dots in each circle; ___1___ dots remaining

3. Share the dots as equally as possible. Draw a picture and write a division statement.

   a) 13 dots in 3 circles   b) 19 dots in 3 circles   c) 36 dots in 5 circles

    13 ÷ 3 = 4 R1

   d) 33 dots in 4 circles   e) 43 dots in 7 circles

4. Eight friends want to share 25 apples among them.
   How many apples will each friend get? 3
   How many will be left over?   25 ÷ 8 =

5. Three siblings have more than 5 and less than 13 animal posters.
   They share the posters evenly with no remainder.
   How many posters do they have? (Show all the possible answers.)

6. Find four different ways to share 19 cookies into equal groups so that one is left over.

each 4 cookies
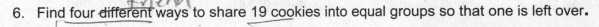
19 ÷ 4 = 4 R 3

TIGER

Number Sense 1

Linda is preparing snacks for four classes.
She needs to divide 95 crackers into 4 groups.
She will use long division and a model to solve the problem.

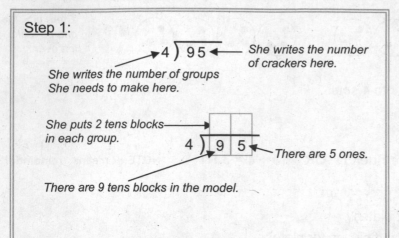

Step 1:

$4 \overline{)95}$

She writes the number of groups She needs to make here.

She writes the number of crackers here.

She puts 2 tens blocks in each group.

$4 \overline{)9 \; 5}$

There are 5 ones.

There are 9 tens blocks in the model.

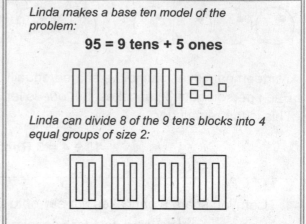

Linda makes a base ten model of the problem:

95 = 9 tens + 5 ones

Linda can divide 8 of the 9 tens blocks into 4 equal groups of size 2:

1. Linda has written a division statement to solve a problem.
   How many groups does she want to make?
   How many tens blocks and how many ones would she need to model the problem?

   a) $2 \overline{)53}$

   groups _____
   tens blocks _____
   ones _____

   b) $5 \overline{)71}$

   groups _____
   tens blocks _____
   ones _____

   c) $4 \overline{)95}$

   groups _____
   tens blocks _____
   ones _____

   d) $5 \overline{)88}$

   groups _____
   tens blocks _____
   ones _____

2. How many tens blocks can be put in each group?

   a) $4 \overline{)5 \; 5}$ b) $5 \overline{)9 \; 7}$ c) $3 \overline{)7 \; 6}$ d) $3 \overline{)8 \; 9}$ e) $4 \overline{)9 \; 2}$

   f) $4 \overline{)4 \; 8}$ g) $5 \overline{)8 \; 7}$ h) $3 \overline{)8 \; 1}$ i) $7 \overline{)8 \; 5}$ j) $8 \overline{)9 \; 6}$

3. For each division statement, write how many groups have been made and how many tens blocks are in each group.

   a) $4 \overline{)8 \; 7}$

   groups _____
   number of tens in each group _____

   b) $3 \overline{)9 \; 4}$

   groups _____
   number of tens in each group _____

   c) $6 \overline{)7 \; 4}$

   groups _____
   number of tens in each group _____

   d) $2 \overline{)9 \; 8}$

   groups _____
   number of tens in each group _____

Step 2:

There are 2 tens blocks in each group.

There are 4 groups.

$2 \times 4 = 8$ tens blocks have been placed.

In the model:

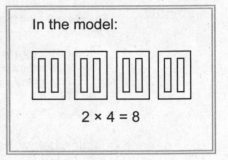

$2 \times 4 = 8$

4. For each question, find how many tens have been placed by multiplying.

a)

How many groups? _____

How many tens? _____

How many tens in each group? _____

How many tens placed altogether? _____

b)

How many groups? _____

How many tens? _____

How many tens in each group? _____.

How many tens placed altogether? _____

5. Use skip counting to find out how many tens can be placed in each group.
   Then use multiplication to find out how many tens have been placed.

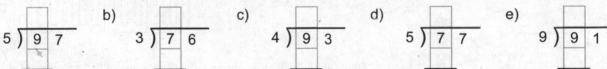

a)　$5 \overline{)9\ 7}$　　b)　$3 \overline{)7\ 6}$　　c)　$4 \overline{)9\ 3}$　　d)　$5 \overline{)7\ 7}$　　e)　$9 \overline{)9\ 1}$

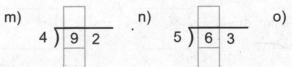

f)　$8 \overline{)9\ 4}$　　g)　$5 \overline{)9\ 4}$　　h)　$2 \overline{)8\ 8}$　　i)　$7 \overline{)9\ 5}$　　j)　$8 \overline{)9\ 9}$

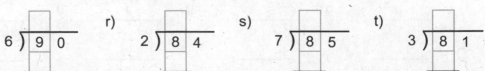

k)　$3 \overline{)8\ 7}$　　l)　$4 \overline{)8\ 5}$　　m)　$4 \overline{)9\ 2}$　　n)　$5 \overline{)6\ 3}$　　o)　$8 \overline{)9\ 6}$

p)　$2 \overline{)9\ 8}$　　q)　$6 \overline{)9\ 0}$　　r)　$2 \overline{)8\ 4}$　　s)　$7 \overline{)8\ 5}$　　t)　$3 \overline{)8\ 1}$

Step 3:

There are 9 tens blocks. Linda has placed 8.

She subtracts to find out how many are left over (9 – 8 = 1).

```
    2
4 ) 9 5
  – 8
    1
```

In the model:

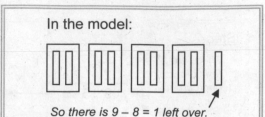

So there is 9 – 8 = 1 left over.

6. For each question below, carry out the first <u>three</u> steps of long division.

a)

```
7 ) 9 7
```

b)

```
3 ) 7 4
```

c)

```
2 ) 6 3
```

d)

```
4 ) 7 3
```

e)

```
6 ) 8 9
```

f)

```
7 ) 8 5
```

g)

```
7 ) 8 4
```

h)

```
3 ) 8 7
```

i)

```
5 ) 7 1
```

j)

```
4 ) 5 2
```

Step 4:

There is one tens block left over and 5 ones. So there are 15 ones left over. Linda writes the 5 beside the 1 to show this.

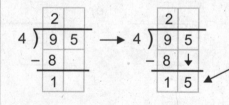

There are this many ones still to place.

In the model:

There are still 15 ones to place in 4 groups.

7. For each question below, carry out the first <u>four</u> steps of long division.

a)

```
5 ) 7 5
  –
```

b)
```
7 ) 8 7
  –
```

c)
```
4 ) 9 3
  –
```

d)
```
2 ) 7 3
  –
```

e)
```
2 ) 7 4
  –
```

f)

```
8 ) 9 7
  –
```

g)

```
4 ) 7 6
  –
```

h)

```
3 ) 9 4
  –
```

i)

```
7 ) 9 1
```

j)

```
9 ) 9 4
```

Step 5:

Linda finds the number of ones he can put in each group by dividing 15 by 4.

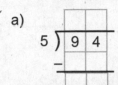

15 ÷ 4 = 3 R = _____

In the model:

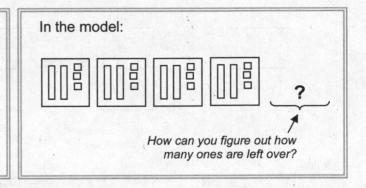

How can you figure out how many ones are left over?

8. For each question below, carry out the first <u>five</u> steps of long division.

a) 5) 9 4

b) 4) 8 7

c) 2) 7 5

d) 3) 5 1

e) 5) 7 2

f) 7) 8 5

g) 2) 9 5

h) 8) 9 6

i) 3) 9 2

j) 2) 9 3

Steps 6 and 7:

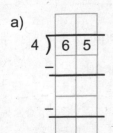

There are 3 ones in each group... and there are 4 groups.

So there are 12 ones altogether in the groups (4 × 3 = 12).

There were 15 ones so there are 3 ones left over (15 – 12 = 3)

In the model:

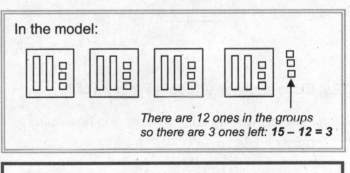

There are 12 ones in the groups so there are 3 ones left: **15 – 12 = 3**

The division statement and the model both show that she can give each class 23 crackers with three left over.

9. For each question below, carry out <u>all seven</u> steps of long division.

a) 4) 6 5

b) 6) 7 8

c) 3) 8 4

d) 3) 7 5

e) 3) 9 6

f)  4) 7 1

g) 5) 8 4

h) 8) 9 6

i) 7) 8 5

j) 9) 9 5

k) 6) 6 9

l) 4) 7 7

m) 9) 9 4

n) 5) 6 8

o) 6) 9 9

10. Alan put 99 sandwiches on platters of 8. How many sandwiches are left over?

11. How many weeks are in 84 days?

12. Elson arranges 97 books into rows of 7.

How many rows can he make and how many books are left over?

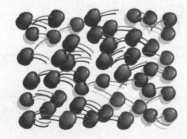

13. Mita spent $91 to rent a canoe for a week.

How much did the canoe cost each day?

14.

Saran divides 59 cherries equally among 4 friends

Wendy divides 74 cherries equally among 5 friends.

Who will have more cherries leftover?

1. Find 313 ÷ 2 by drawing a base ten model and by long division.

   Step 1: Draw a base ten model of 313.

   Draw your model here:

   Step 2: Divide the hundreds blocks into 2 equal groups.

   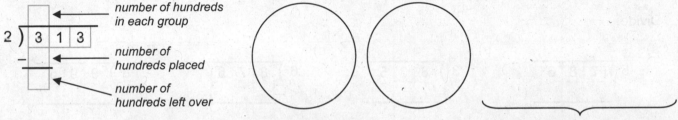

   remaining hundreds, tens and ones

   Step 3: Exchange the left over hundreds block for 10 tens.

   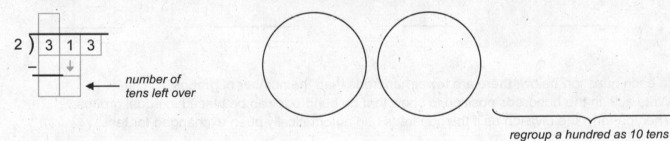

   regroup a hundred as 10 tens

   Step 4: Divide the tens blocks into two equal groups.

   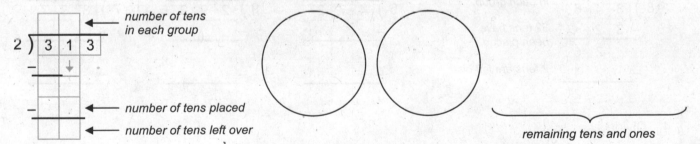

   remaining tens and ones

   Step 5: Exchange the left over tens blocks for 10 ones.

   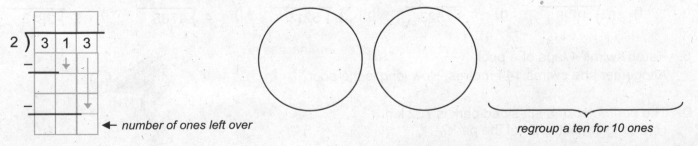

   regroup a ten for 10 ones

<u>Steps 6 and 7</u>: Divide the ones into 2 equal groups.

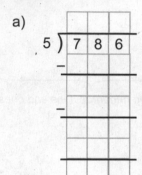

number of ones in each group

$2 \overline{)3\ 1\ 3}$

← number of ones placed
← number of ones left over

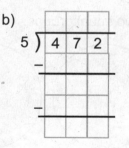
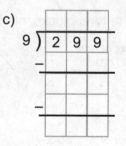
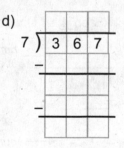

remaining ones

2. Divide.

a) $5 \overline{)7\ 8\ 6}$

b) $3 \overline{)8\ 3\ 5}$

c) $6 \overline{)8\ 7\ 5}$

d) $8 \overline{)9\ 9\ 5}$

3. In each question below, there are fewer hundreds than the number of groups.
Write a '0' in the hundreds position to show that no hundreds can be placed in equal groups.
Then perform the division as if the hundreds had automatically been exchanged for tens.

a)
```
      0 4 3      ← 4 tens can be placed
  8 ) 3 4 6        in each group.
    - 3 2        ← 32 tens have
                    been placed.
        2 6
      - 2 4      ← 2 tens are left over.
          2
```

b) $5 \overline{)4\ 7\ 2}$

c) $9 \overline{)2\ 9\ 9}$

d) $7 \overline{)3\ 6\ 7}$

4. Divide.

a) $3 \overline{)115}$

b) $4 \overline{)341}$

c) $8 \overline{)425}$

d) $6 \overline{)379}$

e) $9 \overline{)658}$

f) $5 \overline{)1525}$

g) $5 \overline{)7523}$

h) $3 \overline{)5213}$

i) $4 \overline{)1785}$

j) $7 \overline{)2213}$

5. Karen swims 4 laps of a pool.
Altogether she swims 144 metres. How long is the pool?

6. The perimeter of a six-sided park is 732 km.
How long is each side of the park?

NS6-37: Topics in Division

1. How many pennies would each friend receive if you divided 3 000 pennies among …

   a) 10 friends? _____   b) 100 friends? _____   c) 1 000 friends? _____

2. Continue the pattern.

   a) $3\,000\,000 \div 10 =$ __300 000__

       $3\,000\,000 \div 100 =$ _____

       $3\,000\,000 \div 1\,000 =$ _____

       $3\,000\,000 \div 10\,000 =$ _____

   b) $2\,700\,000 \div 10 =$ _____

       $2\,700\,000 \div 100 =$ _____

       $2\,700\,000 \div 1\,000 =$ _____

       $2\,700\,000 \div 10\,000 =$ _____

3. Describe any patterns you see in question 2.

4. Under which deal do you pay less for each magazine?

52 Issues
First 4 issues free!
$3 for each issue afterwards

52 Issues
First 12 issues free!
$4 for each issue after that

5. Make up two division questions using the numbers in the chart.

Number of animal stickers in a pack	Price of a pack
8	96 cents
6	78 cents
7	91 cents

In the questions below, you will have to interpret what the remainder means.

> *Example:* Lars wants to put 87 hockey cards into a scrapbook. Each page holds 6 cards.
> How many pages will he need?   **87 ÷ 6 = 14 R3**
> Lars will need **15** pages (because he needs a page for the three leftover cards).

6. 4 people can sleep in a tent.
   How many tents are needed for 58 people?

7. 6 friends share 83 stickers.
   How many stickers does each friend receive?

8. A school cafeteria uses 7 loaves of bread each week.
   In how many weeks and days will the cafeteria use 98 loaves of bread?

9. Esther is moving to a new apartment.
   On each trip her car can carry 6 loads of boxes.
   How many trips will she need to make to move 75 boxes?

Answer the following questions in your notebook.

1.  A bus carries 48 students. How many students can 65 buses carry?

2. If three oranges cost 69¢, how much do nine oranges cost?

3. a) Alice is between 20 and 40 years old. Last year, her age was a multiple of 4. This year, her age is a multiple of 5. How old is Alice?

   b) George is between 30 and 50 years old. Last year, his age was a multiple of 6. This year it is a multiple of 7. How old is George?

4.  A family travelled in a car for 112 days. Gas costs $126 each week.

   How much money did they spend on gas?

5. Can a prime number be divisible by 3? Explain.

6. What is the smallest whole number greater than 100 that is divisible by 99?

7. ☐ 569 ÷ 6 is about 400.

   What digit could be in the box? Explain.

8. Kim buys cherries at a price of 3 for 10¢ and sells the cherries at a price of 5 for 20¢.

   How many cherries does she need to sell to make $1.00?

   HINT: What is the lowest common multiple of 3 and 5?

9. 3 360 trees are planted in 6 rows. How many trees are in each row?

10. There are two adults and two children in the Gordon family.

    The ticket price for a play was $12.50 for adults and $8.50 for children.

    How much money did the family have to pay for the tickets?

    If they received $8 in change, what amount did they pay with?

11. ➤ Choose a number less than 10 and greater than 0.

    ➤ If the number is even, halve it and add one. If the number is odd, double it.

    ➤ Again, if the new number is even, halve it and add one. If the new number is odd, double it.

    a) Continue the number snake for the example. What happens?

    b) Investigate which one-digit number makes the longest snake.

    c) Try starting a number snake with a two-digit number. What happens?

    > *Example:*
    > 9
    > 9 → 18
    > 9 → 18 → 10

1. Draw an arrow to the 0 or 10 to show whether the circled number is closer to **0 or 10**.

a)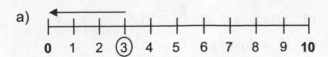

b)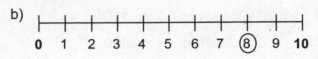

c)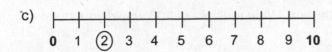

d)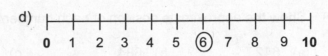

2. a) Which one-digit numbers are closer to i) 0? _____   ii) 10? _____

   b) Why is 5 a special case? _____

3. Draw an arrow to show which multiple of ten you would round to.

   Then round each number to the nearest tens.

a)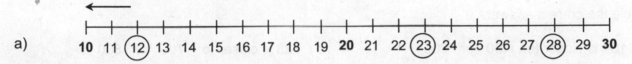

   Round to ___10___ _____ _____

b)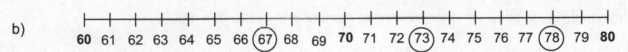

   Round to _____ _____ _____

c)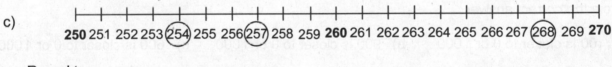

   Round to _____ _____ _____

4. Circle the correct answer.

   a) 21 is closer to 20 or 30   b) 12 is closer to 10 or 20

   c) 38 is closer to 30 or 40   d) 75 is closer to 70 or 80

   e) 252 is closer to 250 or 260   f) 586 is closer to 580 or 590

5. Draw an arrow to show whether the circled number is closer to 0 or 100.

a)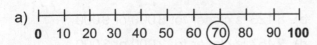

b)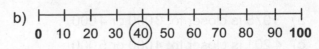

6. Is 50 closer to 0 or to 100? Why is 50 a special case?

_____

7. Circle the correct answer.

     a) 70 is closer to: 0   or   100   b) 30 is closer to: 0   or   100

     c) 60 is closer to: 0   or   100   d) 10 is closer to: 0   or   100

8. Show the approximate position of each number on the line. What multiple of 100 would you round to?

     a)   642   b)   684   c)   793   d)   701

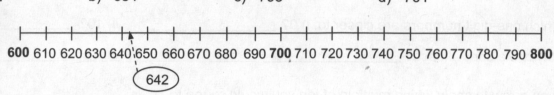

     Round to   _____

9. Circle the correct answer.

     a) 164 is closer to: 100   or   200   b) 723 is closer to: 700   or   800

     c) 678 is closer to: 600   or   700   d) 957 is closer to: 900   or   1 000

10. Draw an arrow to show whether the circled number is closer to 0 or 1 000.

     a) 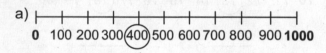   b)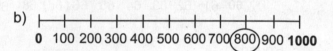

11. Circle the correct answer.

     a)   100 is closer to 0 or 1 000   b)   900 is closer to 0 or 1 000   c)   600 is closer to 0 or 1 000

12. Draw an arrow to show which multiple of 1000 you would round to.

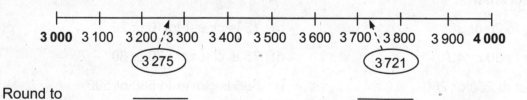

     Round to   _____   _____

13. Circle the correct answer.

     a)   3 975 is closer to: 3 000 or 4 000   b)   8 123 is closer to: 8 000 or 9 000

     c)   4 201 is closer to: 4 000 or 5 000   d)   2 457 is closer to: 2 000 or 3 000

 14. Write a rule for rounding a four-digit number to the nearest thousands.

NS6-40: Rounding

1. Round to the nearest <u>tens</u> place.

   a) 38 [ ]   b) 46 [ ]

   c) 21 [ ]   d) 62 [ ]

   e) 79 [ ]   f) 81 [ ]

   g) 25 [ ]   h) 36 [ ]   i) 91 [ ]

   > **REMEMBER:**
   >
   > If the number in the ones digit is:
   >
   > 0, 1, 2, 3 or 4 – you round <u>down</u>
   >
   > 5, 6, 7, 8 or 9 – you round <u>up</u>

2. Round to the nearest <u>tens</u> place. Underline the tens digit first. Then put your pencil on the digit to the right (the ones digit). This digit tells you whether to round up or down.

   a) 6<u>5</u>6 [660]   b) 273 [ ]   c) 152 [ ]

   d) 355 [ ]   e) 418 [ ]   f) 566 [ ]

   g) 128 [ ]   h) 467 [ ]   i) 338 [ ]

3. Round the following numbers to the nearest <u>hundreds</u> place. Underline the hundreds digit first. Then put your pencil on the digit to the right (the tens digit).

   a) <u>3</u>40 [300]   b) 490 [ ]   c) 570 [ ]

   d) 270 [ ]   e) 160 [ ]   f) 360 [ ]

   g) 460 [ ]   h) 840 [ ]   i) 980 [ ]

4. Round the following numbers to the nearest <u>hundreds</u> place. As in the last question, underline the hundreds digit first. Then put your pencil on the digit to the right (the tens digit).

   a) 167 [ ]   b) 347 [ ]   c) 567 [ ]

   d) 349 [ ]   e) 873 [ ]   f) 291 [ ]

5. Round the following numbers to the nearest <u>thousands</u> place. Underline the thousands digit first. Then put your pencil on the digit to the right (the hundreds digit).

   a) <u>4</u> 787 [5 000]   b) 3 092 [ ]   c) 7 697 [ ]

   d) 5 021 [ ]   e) 2 723 [ ]   f) 8 538 [ ]

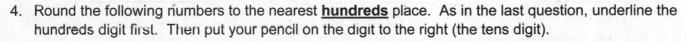

jump math
MULTIPLYING POTENTIAL

Number Sense 1

6. Underline the digit you wish to round to. Then say whether you would round up or down.

a) *hundreds*

7	3	2	5

round up
~~round down~~ (circled)

b) *hundreds*

4	1	2	7

round up
round down

c) *tens*

4	9	6	3

round up
round down

d) *thousands*

8	3	8	6	4

round up
round down

e) *ten thousands*

4	6	5	2	3

round up
round down

f) *ten thousands*

1	2	5	5	9

round up
round down

7. Complete the two steps from question 6. Then follow the two steps below.

Round the digit underlined up or down.

- To round up add 1 to the digit.
- To round down keep the digit the same.

7	3	4	5
	3		

ru
(rd) circled

The digits to the right of the rounded digit become zeroes.

The digits to the left remain the same.

7	3	4	5
7	3	0	0

ru
(rd) circled

a) *thousands*

7	2	1	0	3

ru
rd

b) *ten thousands*

9	3	5	6	8

ru
rd

c) *hundreds*

8	4	2	1	3

ru
rd

d) *hundreds*

2	7	5	1	3

ru
rd

e) *tens*

4	6	1	2	7	3

ru
rd

f) *tens thousands*

1	4	2	3	7	5

ru
rd

8. Sometimes in rounding, you have to regroup.

Example:
Round 3995 to the
nearest hundred.

3	9	8	5
	10		

900 rounds to 1000.

3	9	8	5
4	0		

*Regroup the 10 hundreds
as 1 (thousand) and add
it to the 3 (thousand).*

3	9	8	5
4	0	0	0

Complete the rounding.

 Round each number to the digit given (regroup if necessary).

a) 3 293   *tens*

b) 5 921   *hundreds*

c) 9 723   *thousands*

d) 13 975   *tens*

e) 23 159   *hundreds*

f) 999 857   *ten thousands*

g) 395 321   *hundred thousands*

1. Estimate the sums and differences.

≈ ← Mathematicians use this symbol to mean **"approximately equal to"**.

a) 42 ⟶ [40]   b) 28 ⟶ [ ]   c) 62 ⟶ [ ]   d) 87 ⟶ [ ]
    + 23 ⟶ + [20]   + 54 ⟶ + [ ]   − 19 ⟶ − [ ]   − 57 ⟶ − [ ]
         [60]

e) 73 + 17 ≈ __70 + 20 = 90__   f) 89 − 46 ≈ _____   g) 16 + 34 ≈ _____

h) 63 + 26 ≈ _____   i) 82 + 47 ≈ _____   j) 46 − 17 ≈ _____

k) 48 + 27 ≈ _____   l) 76 + 14 ≈ _____   m) 92 − 38 ≈ _____

2. Estimate by rounding to the nearest hundreds.

a) 290 ⟶ [300]   b) 390 ⟶ [ ]   c) 630 ⟶ [ ]   d) 840 ⟶ [ ]
    + 360 ⟶ + [400]   + 460 ⟶ + [ ]   − 170 ⟶ − [ ]   − 550 ⟶ − [ ]
         [700]

e) 680 + 160 ≈ _____   f) 470 − 220 ≈ _____

g) 610 + 240 ≈ _____   h) 840 + 180 ≈ _____

i) 670 + 340 ≈ _____   j) 941 − 463 ≈ _____

k) 126 + 567 ≈ _____   l) 523 + 285 ≈ _____

BONUS
3. To estimate, round to the nearest thousands or ten thousands.

a) 1 275 ⟶ [1000]   b) 4 729 ⟶ [ ]   c) 2 570 ⟶ [ ]   d) 29 753 ⟶ [ ]
    + 3 940 ⟶ + [4000]   − 3 132 ⟶ − [ ]   + 6 234 ⟶ + [ ]   − 23 123 ⟶ − [ ]
         [5 000]

4. Round to the nearest hundreds then find the sum or difference.

a) 3 272 + 1 976   b) 3 581 − 1 926   c) 64 857 − 42 345

jump math
MULTIPLYING POTENTIAL.

Number Sense 1

1. The population of Saskatchewan is 995 000 and the population of New Brunswick is 750 500.

   Estimate the difference in the two populations.

Saskatchewan   **New Brunswick**

2. The population of Newfoundland is 520 200 and the population of Prince Edward Island is 137 900.

   Estimate the total population of the two provinces.

Newfoundland   **Prince Edward Island**

3. Round 628 315 to the nearest

   a) tens

   b) hundreds

   c) thousands

   d) ten thousands

4. Estimate the products by rounding to the leading digits.

   a) 32 × 75

   b) 492 × 81

   c) 307 × 12

   d) 2 759 × 812

5. Estimate the following total amounts.

   a) 6 tapes at $4.99 a tape

   b) 5 pies at $3.12 a pie

   c) 8 books at $7.87 a book

6. Jacques multiplied a 1-digit number by a 3-digit number. The product was about 1 000.

   Describe three different pairs of numbers he might have multiplied.

7. The populations of New Brunswick and Nova Scotia are listed in an almanac as 750 000 and 936 900.

   What digit do you think these numbers have been rounded to? Explain.

   Nova Scotia

8. There are 1 483 beads in a jar.

   It takes 58 beads to make a bracelet.

   Sandra estimates that she can make 30 bracelets.

   Is her estimate reasonable? Explain.

9. A supermarket sold 472 apples, 783 oranges, 341 pears and 693 bananas.

   a) How many pieces of fruit did they sell in all?

   b) Use estimation to check your solution. Explain your estimation strategy.

10. To estimate the difference 1 875 – 1 432, should you round the numbers to the nearest thousands or the nearest hundreds? Explain.

Answer the questions in your notebook

1. Predict which range each product or quotient will lie in before you perform the calculation.

A. 1 to 10	**B.** 11 to 100	**C.** 101 to 500	**D.** 501 to 1 000	**E.** above 1 000

   a) 37 × 25   b) 4 279 ÷ 70   c) 13 200 ÷ 600   d) 45 × 87

2. Which method of estimation will work best for each calculation below? Justify your answers.

   • Rounding   • Front-end estimation (round both numbers down to the leading digit)
   • Rounding one number up and one number down

   a) 657 + 452   b) 891 + 701   c) 425 + 375   d) 395 − 352

   For which question does neither method work well?

3. Use any method of estimation you choose to judge whether the answer is reasonable.
   Then perform the calculation to check if the answer is correct.

   a) 3 875 + 2 100 = 8 257   b) 37 × 435 = 1 285   c) 9 352 − 276 = 9 076

4. Some calculations are easy because …

You can group numbers that add to 10 or 100.	You can do the calculation in steps.	You don't have to regroup.
$4(7) + 3(3) + 5(40) + 3(60)$	$100 - 23$ $= 100 - 20 - 3$	$3 × 213 = 639$

   Which calculations below could you do mentally? Describe your method.
   For the harder calculations, say how you would estimate.

   a) 3 875 − 1 325   b) 800 − 53   c) 876 × 9   d) 7 521 + 9 859

   e) 532 × 3   f) 321 + 587 + 413 + 379   g) 42 000 ÷ 70

5. Write a number that could be rounded to:

   a) 1 000 or 1 400.

   b) 6 000 or 5 900 or 5 870.

6. How would you estimate …

   a) the length of a row of 10 000 loonies?

   b) the number of seconds in a year?

1. Complete each pattern by counting by the first number given, then by the following numbers given.

a)
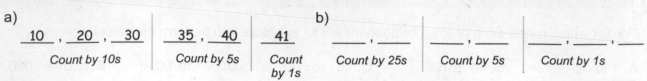

10 , 20 , 30	35 , 40	41
Count by 10s	Count by 5s	Count by 1s

b)

___ , ___	___ , ___	___ , ___ , ___
Count by 25s	Count by 5s	Count by 1s

c)
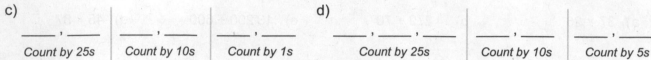

___ , ___	___ , ___	___ , ___
Count by 25s	Count by 10s	Count by 1s

d)

___ , ___ , ___	___ , ___	___ , ___
Count by 25s	Count by 10s	Count by 5s

e)
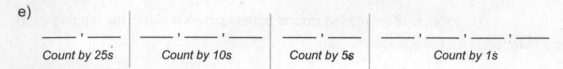

___ , ___	___ , ___ , ___	___ , ___	___ , ___ , ___ , ___
Count by 25s	Count by 10s	Count by 5s	Count by 1s

2. Write the total amount of money in cents for the number of coins given in the charts below.
   HINT: Count by the greater amount first.

a)

Nickels	Pennies
6	7

Total amount =

b)

Quarters	Dimes
3	2

Total amount =

c)

Quarters	Nickels
5	5

Total amount =

BONUS

d)

Quarters	Nickels	Pennies
4	2	4

Total amount =

e)

Quarters	Nickels	Pennies
6	3	7

Total amount =

f)

Quarters	Dimes	Nickels	Pennies
2	3	1	5

Total amount =

g)

Quarters	Dimes	Nickels	Pennies
5	2	2	2

Total amount =

3. Count the given coins and write the total amount in cents.
   HINT: Count by the greater amount first.

a) Total amount =

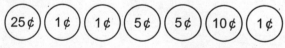
25¢ 1¢ 1¢ 5¢ 5¢ 10¢ 1¢

b) Total amount =

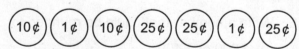
10¢ 1¢ 10¢ 25¢ 25¢ 1¢ 25¢

c) Total amount =

10¢ 1¢ 25¢ 5¢ 10¢ 25¢ 10¢

d) Total amount =

5¢ 10¢ 25¢ 5¢ 1¢ 5¢ 25¢

BONUS
e) Total amount =

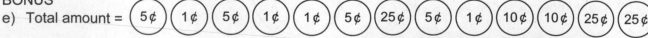
5¢ 1¢ 5¢ 1¢ 1¢ 5¢ 25¢ 5¢ 1¢ 10¢ 10¢ 25¢ 25¢

1. Draw in the number of <u>additional</u> coins needed to make each total.

a)   (10¢) (10¢)   How many dimes?   = 40¢

b)   (25¢) (5¢)   How many quarters?   = 80¢

c)   (25¢) (25¢)   How many dimes?   = 80¢

d)   (25¢) (5¢)   How many quarters?   = 55¢

2. Draw the <u>additional</u> coins needed to make each total. must use **two** extra coins for each question.

a) 16¢ (10¢)	b) 60¢ (25¢) (5¢)	
c) 50¢ (25¢) (10¢)	d) 80¢ (25¢) (25¢)	
e) 41¢ (10¢) (1¢)	f) 65¢ (25¢) (25¢)	
g) 95¢ (25¢) (25¢) (25¢)	h) 90¢ (25¢) (25¢) (25¢)	
i) $4 ($2)	j) $7 ($2) ($2)	
k) $5 ($1)	l) $8 ($2) ($2) ($1)	
m) 136¢ ($1) (10¢)	n) 331¢ ($2) ($1) (25¢)	

3. Draw a picture to show the extra coins each child will need to pay for the item they want.

a) Ron has 35¢. He wants to buy an eraser for 65¢.

b) Alan has 3 quarters, a dime, and a nickel. He wants to buy a sandwich for 98¢.

c) Jane has 3 toonies and a loonie. She wants to buy a skirt for ten dollars.

d) Raiz has 4 toonies and 2 loonies. He wants to buy a book for eleven dollars and sixty-five cents.

4. Lyubava makes $4.00 using 10 coins. Find 2 possible sets of coins she could have used.

5. Make up a problem like one of the problems in Question 3 and exchange it with a classmate to solve.

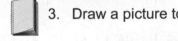

jump math
MULTIPLYING POTENTIAL.

Number Sense 1

1. What is the greatest amount you could pay in quarters without exceeding the amount? Draw the quarters to show your answer.

	Amount	Greatest amount you could pay in quarters:		Amount	Greatest amount you could pay in quarters:
a)	55¢		b)	56¢	
c)	89¢		d)	77¢	
e)	43¢		f)	65¢	
g)	39¢		h)	24¢	
i)	83¢		j)	96¢	

2. Find the greatest amount you could pay in quarters. Represent the amount remaining using the least number of coins.

	Amount	Amount Paid in Quarters	Amount Remaining	Amount Remaining in Coins
a)	84¢	75¢	84¢ - 75¢ = 9¢	5¢ 1¢ 1¢ 1¢ 1¢
b)	67¢			
c)	86¢			
d)	91¢			

3. Trade coins to make each amount with the least amount of coins.
   Draw a picture to show your answer.

a) 5¢ 5¢ 10¢ 10¢   b) 25¢ 25¢ 25¢ 25¢   c) 5¢ 5¢ 5¢ $1

d) 10¢ 10¢ 10¢ $1   e) 25¢ 5¢ 10¢ 10¢ 25¢ $1 25¢ 25¢

f) 10¢ 10¢ 5¢ $1 10¢ $2 $1 10¢ 1¢ 1¢ 5¢ 5¢

4. Show how you could trade the amounts for the least number of coins.

a) 7 quarters   b) 5 dimes and 3 nickels   c) 8 loonies

d) 9 loonies and 6 dimes   e) 8 loonies, 6 dimes, 3 nickels and 5 pennies

5. Find the number of coins you need to make the amount in the right-hand column of the chart.

   HINT: Count up by quarters until you are as close to the amount as possible. Then count on by dimes, and so on.

	Number of Quarters	Subtotal	Number of Dimes	Subtotal	Number of Nickels	Subtotal	Number of Pennies	Total Amount
a)	3	75¢	0	75¢	1	80¢	3	83¢
b)								64¢
c)								86¢
d)								22¢
e)								48¢
f)								92¢

6. Write the greatest amount you could pay in $20 bills, without exceeding the amount.

   a) $45 = __$40__   b) $33 = _____   c) $25 = _____   d) $51 = _____   e) $67 = _____

7. Write the number (#) of each type of bill or coin you would need to get the amounts given.

	#	Type	#	Type	#	Type	#	Type	#	Type	#	Type
a) $21.00	0	$50.00	1	$20.00	0	$10.00	0	$5.00	0	$2.00	1	$1.00
b) $35.00		$50.00		$20.00		$10.00		$5.00		$2.00		$1.00
c) $52.00		$50.00		$20.00		$10.00		$5.00		$2.00		$1.00
d) $88.00		$50.00		$20.00		$10.00		$5.00		$2.00		$1.00
e) $66.00		$50.00		$20.00		$10.00		$5.00		$2.00		$1.00

8. In your notebook, draw the least number of coins you need to make the following amounts.

   a) 75¢   b) 46¢   c) 81¢   d) 96¢

9. Draw the least number of coins and bills you would need to make the following amounts.

   a) $55.00   b) $68.00   c) $72.00   d) $125.00

   e) $62.35   f) $43.13   g) $57.81   h) $71.12

   i) $63.06   j) $158.50   k) $92.83   l) $35.23

NS6-47: Dollar and Cent Notation

1. Write the given amount in dollars, dimes and pennies, then in dollar notation.

Amount in ¢	Dollars	Dimes	Pennies	Amount in $	Amount in ¢	Dollars	Dimes	Pennies	Amount in $
a) 173¢	1	7	3	$ 1.73	b) 372¢				
c) 37¢					d) 8¢				

2. Change the amount to cent notation, then dollar notation.

a) 7 pennies = __7¢__ = __$ .07__   b) 6 nickels = _____ = _____   c) 9 dimes = _____ = _____

d) 3 pennies = _____ = _____   e) 11 pennies = _____ = _____   f) 1 quarter = _____ = _____

g) 4 nickels = _____ = _____   h) 7 quarters = _____ = _____   i) 8 dimes = _____ = _____

j) 5 toonies = _____ = _____   k) 8 loonies = _____ = _____   l) 2 loonies = _____ = _____

3. Count the dollar amount and the cent amount. Write the total amount in dollar (decimal) notation.

	Dollar Amount	Cent Amount	Total
a)	$2 $1 $1 = _____	25¢ 25¢ 5¢ = _____	_____
b)	20 5 = _____	25¢ 10¢ 5¢ = _____	_____
c)	10 10 = _____	25¢ 25¢ 1¢ = _____	_____

4. Count the given coins. Write the total amount in cents and in dollars (decimals).

Coins	Cent Notation	Dollar Notation
a) 25¢ 25¢ 25¢ 25¢ 5¢	105¢	$1.05
b) 25¢ 25¢ 25¢ 10¢ 10¢ 10¢ 1¢	_____	_____

5. Write each number of cents in dollar notation.

a) 437¢ = _____   b) 40¢ = _____   c) 5¢ = _____   d) 348¢ = _____   e) 306¢ = _____

jump math
MULTIPLYING POTENTIAL

Number Sense 1

6. Write each amount of money in cent notation.

    a) $2.39 = _____   b) $5.53 = _____   c) $6.41 = _____   d) $0.06 = _____

7. Circle the greater amount of money in each pair.

    a)   293¢   or $2.96   b) $1.05   or   107¢   c)   7¢   or $0.70

    d) $6.85   or   686¢   e)   640¢   or $6.04   f) $0.23   or   122¢

8. Circle the larger amount of money in each pair.

    a)   seven dollars and fifty-five cents   or   seven dollars and seventy cents

    b)   nine dollars and eighty-three cents   or   978¢

    c)   fifteen dollars and forty cents   or $15.08

9. Tally the amount of each type of denomination then find the total.

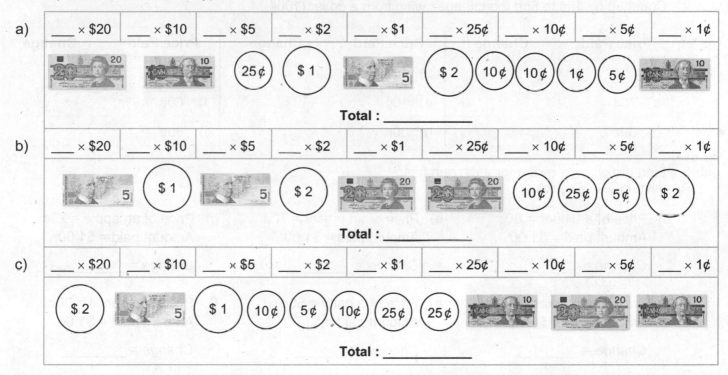

10. Which is a greater amount of money: $427 or $4.32? Explain how you know.

11. Ken paid for an eraser with 5 coins. The eraser cost 85¢. Which coins did he use?

12. Myles bought a pack of cards for $4.50. He paid for it with 4 coins. Which coins did he use?

13. Tanya's weekly allowance is $10.25. Her mom gave her 8 coins. Which coins did she use?

14. Write words for the following amounts.

    a) $4.85   b) $13.24   c) $8.25   d) $461.99   e) $385.99   f) $4 523.02

1. Calculate the change owing for each purchase. Subtract the amounts by counting up on your fingers if necessary.

   a) Price of a pencil = 44¢
      Amount paid = 50¢

      Change = _____

   b) Price of an eraser = 41¢
      Amount paid = 50¢

      Change = _____

   c) Price of a sharpener = 84¢
      Amount paid = 90¢

      Change = _____

   d) Price of a ruler = 53¢
      Amount paid = 60¢

      Change = _____

   e) Price of a marker = 76¢
      Amount paid = 80¢

      Change = _____

   f) Price of a notebook = 65¢
      Amount paid = 70¢

      Change = _____

   g) Price of a folder = 68¢
      Amount paid = 70¢

      Change = _____

   h) Price of a juice box = 49¢
      Amount paid = 50¢

      Change = _____

   i) Price of a freezie = 28¢
      Amount paid = 30¢

      Change = _____

2. Count up by 10s to find the change owing from a dollar (100¢).

Price Paid	Change	Price Paid	Change	Price Paid	Change
a) 90¢		b) 40¢		c) 20¢	
d) 70¢		e) 10¢		f) 60¢	
g) 50¢		h) 30¢		i) 80¢	

3. Find the change owing for each purchase.
   HINT: Count up by 10s.

   a) Price of a binder = 80¢
      Amount paid = $1.00

      Change = _____

   b) Price of an eraser = 70¢
      Amount paid = $1.00

      Change = _____

   c) Price of an apple = 20¢
      Amount paid = $1.00

      Change = _____

   d) Price of a marker = 60¢
      Amount paid = $1.00

      Change = _____

   e) Price of a patty = 50¢
      Amount paid = $1.00

      Change = _____

   f) Price of a pencil = 30¢
      Amount paid = $1.00

      Change = _____

   g) Price of a sharpener = 10¢
      Amount paid = $1.00

      Change = _____

   h) Price of juice = 40¢
      Amount paid = $1.00

      Change = _____

   i) Price of a popsicle = 60¢
      Amount paid = $1.00

      Change = _____

4. Find the smallest two-digit number ending in zero (i.e. 10, 20, 30, 40...) that is <u>greater</u> than the number given. Write your answer in the box provided.

   a) 74 [80]   b) 56 [ ]   c) 43 [ ]   d) 28 [ ]   e) 57 [ ]   f) 4 [ ]

Step 1:   Find the smallest multiple of 10 greater than 16¢.   16¢ → 20¢

Step 2:   Find the differences: 20 – 16 and 100 - 20   16¢ —4→ 20¢ —80→ 100¢

Step 3:   Add the differences: 4¢ + 80¢   **Change = 84¢**

5.   Make change for the number written below. Follow the steps shown above.

a)

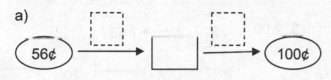

Change = _____

b)

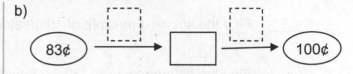

Change = _____

c)

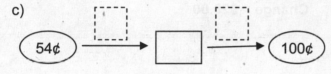

Change = _____

d)

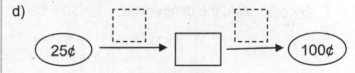

Change = _____

e)

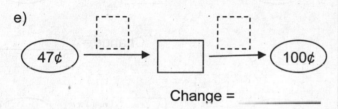

Change = _____

f)

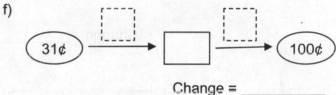

Change = _____

6.   Find change from 100¢ for the following. Try to do the work in your head.

a) 74¢ _____   b) 47¢ _____   c) 36¢ _____   d) 53¢ _____   e) 72¢ _____

f) 35¢ _____   g) 97¢ _____   h) 59¢ _____   i) 89¢ _____   j) 92¢ _____

7.   Find the change for the following amount in your head.

a)   Price: 37¢   Amount Paid: 50¢   b)   Price: 58¢   Amount Paid: 75¢

    Change Required: _____   Change Required: _____

8.   Paul paid for a 42¢ stamp with $1.00. How much change should he get back?
    Draw the amount of change using the least number of coins.

9. Find the change.

Amount Paid	Price	Change	Amount Paid	Price	Change
a) $30.00	$22.00		d) $70.00	$64.00	
b) $40.00	$34.00		e) $90.00	$87.00	
c) $50.00	$44.00		f) $20.00	$12.00	

10. Make change for the amount written below. Follow the steps shown for finding the change from $50.00 on a payment of $22.00.

Step 1: Find the smallest multiple of 10 greater than $22.00. $22 → $30

Step 2: Find the differences: 30 – 22 and 50 – 30 $22 →⁸ $30 →²⁰ $50

Step 3: Add the differences: $8 + $20   **Change = $28.00**

a)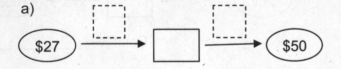

Change = _____

b)

$38 → → $100

Change = _____

c)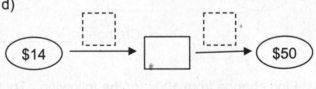

$53 → → $100

Change = _____

d)

$14 → → $50

Change = _____

11. Find the change from $100 for the following. Try to do the work in your head.

a) $84 = _____   b) $25 = _____   c) $46 = _____   d) $88 = _____   e) $52 _____

12. Find the change by first finding the change from the nearest dollar amount and then the change from the nearest multiples of 10.

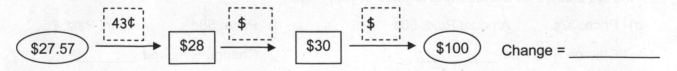

$27.57 →⁴³¢ $28 →$ $30 →$ $100   Change = _____

13. Using the method of Question 12, find the change from $100 for the following amounts in your notebook.

a) $32.85   b) $86.27   c) $52.19   d) $66.43

1. Sara spent $14.32 on a cake and $4.27 on candles. To find out how much she spent, she added the amounts using the following steps.

<u>Step 1:</u>
She lined up the numerals: she put dollars above dollars, dimes above dimes and pennies above pennies:

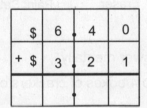

	$	1	4 .	3	2
+	$		4 .	2	7

<u>Step 2:</u>
She added the numerals, starting with the ones digits (the pennies):

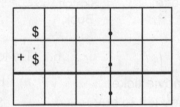

	$	1	4 .	3	2
+	$		4 .	2	7
					9

<u>Step 3:</u>
She added a decimal to show the amount in dollars:

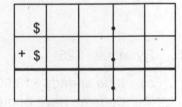

	$	1	4 .	3	2
+	$		4 .	2	7
		1	8 .	5	9

Add.

a) $6.40 + $3.21

	$	6 .	4	0
+	$	3 .	2	1

b) $37.25 + $41.32

	$	.		
+	$	.		
		.		

c) $18.34 + $21.63

	$	.		
+	$	.		
		.		

2. In order to add the amounts below, you will have to regroup.

a)

	$	2	7 .	5	0
+	$	3	4 .	8	6

b)

	$	3	8 .	3	4
+	$	5	4 .	2	1

c)

	$	9	8 .	3	2
+	$		7 .	4	3

d)

	$	4	2 .	3	9
+	$	8	4 .	0	5

e)

	$	9	3 .	1	2
+	$	5	5 .	3	6

f)

	$	2	6 .	3	0
+	$	8	9 .	2	3

 Solve the following word problems in your notebook.

3. a) Jasmine bought a science kit for $32.27 and a microscope for $73.70. How much money does she need to pay for the items?

b) A school spent $527.32 on books and $632.50 on other supplies. How much did the school spend in total?

c) Amy bought three plants that cost $17.25 each. How much did she pay in total?

Answer the following questions in your notebook.

4. a) If you bought an easel and paint set, how much would you pay?

   b) Which costs more: (i) a paint set and a palette, or (ii) a frame, a sketch book and an eraser?

   c) You have $27. Do you have enough money to buy the brush, palette and frame?

   d) You have $100. How much more do you need to buy everything?

   e) Make up your own problem using the items.

$59.95	$5.50	$19.95	$9.90	$5.99	$0.99	$4.95
Easel	Brush	Palette	Sketch Book	Frame	Eraser	Paint Set

5. Ryan has $25.

   a) If he spends $13.00 for a movie ticket, does he have enough money left to buy popcorn and a pop, which cost $7.75?

   b) If he buys a board game for $9.50 and a comic book for $10.35, will he have enough money left to buy a book which costs $5.10?

6. Try to find the answer mentally.

   a) How much do 4 boxes of crackers cost at $3.20 each?

   b) How many pears, costing 60¢ each, could you buy with $5.00?

   c) Paint brushes cost $4.05. How many could you buy if you had $25.00?

   d) Is $100.00 enough to pay for a book costing $40.75 and a sweater costing $59.37?

   e) Which costs more: 4 skate boards at $225.00 each or 3 snowboards at $310.00 dollars each?

7. How many of each bill would you need to make $10 000.00?

   a) A hundred dollar bill
   b) A fifty dollar bill
   c) A twenty dollar bill

   Explain how you can use your answer to (a) to answer (b) and (c).

8. Show all the ways you can make $100 using five dollar, ten dollar and twenty dollar bills.

1. Find the remaining amount by subtracting.

a)
$	5	. 7	3
– $	3	. 4	0

b)
$	7	. 5	4
– $	3	. 1	2

c)
$	9	. 8	9
– $	4	. 2	3

d)
$	7	. 0	5
– $	2	. 0	4

e)
$	7	. 9	3
– $	6	. 3	2

2. Subtract the given money amounts by regrouping.

Example:

Step 1:
	6	10	
$	7̸	0̸	0
– $	2	4	3

Step 2:
	6	9 / 10	10
$	7̸	0̸	0
– $	2	4	3

a)
$	5	. 0	0
– $	3	. 7	8

b)
$	8	. 0	0
– $	5	. 3	3

c)
$	9	. 0	0
– $	4	. 5	8

d)
$	6	2	. 0	0
– $	3	1	. 2	9

e)
$	4	5	. 5	0
– $	3	8	. 3	9

f)
$	8	8	. 3	7
– $	2	4	. 8	3

3. George paid for a telescope that costs $275.50 with three hundred dollar bills. Calculate his change.

4. Mera has $275.32 and Wendy has $42.53. How much more money does Mera have than Wendy?

5. A school spent $1387.25 on uniforms. The boys' uniforms cost $723.05.

   How much did the girls' uniforms cost?

6. Mark has $50.00.

   He wants to buy a pair of shoes that cost $23.52 and a pair of pants that costs $39.47.

   How much more money does he need to buy the pants and shoes?

NS6-51: Estimation

1. For each collection of coins and bills estimate the amount to the nearest dollar and then count the precise amount.

a)

___ × $20	___ × $10	___ × $5	___ × $2	___ × $1	___ × 25¢	___ × 10¢	___ × 5¢	___ × 1¢

10   10   10¢ $2   5 $2   10¢ $2   1¢   5¢   20

Estimate: _____   Total : _____

b)

___ × $20	___ × $10	___ × $5	___ × $2	___ × $1	___ × 25¢	___ × 10¢	___ × 5¢	___ × 1¢

10¢ $1 $1   10 $2   20   20   10¢   25¢   5¢   25¢

1¢   10   10   Estimate: _____   Total : _____

c)

___ × $20	___ × $10	___ × $5	___ × $2	___ × $1	___ × 25¢	___ × 10¢	___ × 5¢	___ × 1¢

$2   5 $1   1¢   5¢   1¢   25¢   25¢   10   20   10

20   10¢   1¢   10   Estimate: _____   Total : _____

2. Round the given cent amounts to the nearest tens place. The first one has been done for you.

a) 74¢   [70¢]

b) 53¢   [ ]

c) 92¢   [ ]

d) 26¢   [ ]

e) 31¢   [ ]

f) 12¢   [ ]

g) 87¢   [ ]

h) 19¢   [ ]

i) 45¢   [ ]

> **REMEMBER:**
> If the number in the <u>ones</u> digit is:
> **0, 1, 2, 3 or 4** – you round **down**
> **5, 6, 7, 8 or 9** – you round **up**

3. Circle the amount where the <u>cent</u> amount is less than 50¢. The first one has been done for you.

a) (̶$̶6̶.̶2̶7̶)   b) $7.82   c) $9.63   d) $6.38   e) $8.05   f) $3.99

27 is less than 50

4. Round the given amounts to the nearest dollar amount.

a) $6.82   [ ]

b) $37.88   [ ]

c) $4.09   [ ]

d) $99.52   [ ]

e) $25.50   [ ]

f) $59.30   [ ]

g) $365.23   [ ]

h) $17.23   [ ]

i) $123.89   [ ]

j) $128.37   [ ]

> **REMEMBER:**
> If the cent amount is <u>less than</u> 50¢, you round **down**.
> If the cent amount is <u>equal to</u> or <u>more than</u> 50¢, you round **up**.

5. Estimate the following sums and differences by rounding each amount to the nearest dollar amount. Then perform the calculation. Does your answer to the calculation seem reasonable?

a) $4.35
    + $4.65

b) $7.66
    − $3.26

c) $5.81
    + $3.37

d) $9.85
    − $2.67

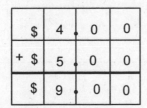 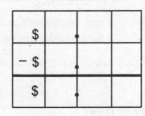 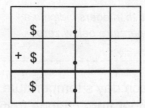 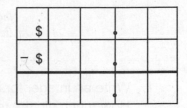

e) $26.83
    − $15.56

f) $57.64
    + $20.35

g) $75.47
    + $17.22

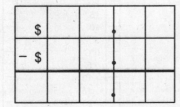 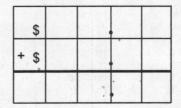 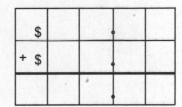

6. Chloe has $100.

    She bought a dog for $59.70.

    Estimate her change.

7. Kim bought two tickets to the museum for $22.58 each.

    She paid with a $50.00 bill.

    Estimate her change.

8. Pamela bought three books that cost $28.82 each.

    About how much money did she spend?

9. Explain why rounding to the nearest dollar isn't helpful for the following question.

    "Hannah has $39.47. Ali has $38.74"

    About how much more money does Hannah have than Ali?"

10. For each problem below, make an estimate and then find the exact amount.

    a) Emma has $127.50. Don has $118.73. How much more money does Emma have than Don?

    b) Marcel has $1520.15. Shawn has $357.80. How much money do they have altogether?

Temperature is recorded on a scale that includes **negative** and **positive** whole numbers.

These numbers are called **integers**.

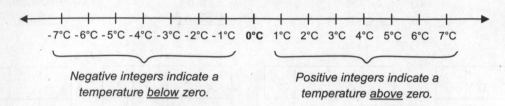

Negative integers indicate a temperature _below_ zero.

Positive integers indicate a temperature _above_ zero.

---

1. Write an integer for each day's temperature.
   How much did the temperature change from day to day?
   (If the temperature fell, write a negative sign in front of your answer)

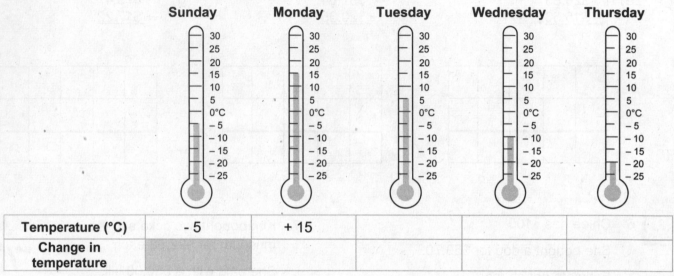

	Sunday	Monday	Tuesday	Wednesday	Thursday
Temperature (°C)	– 5	+ 15			
Change in temperature					

2.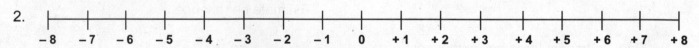

   a) Mark the numbers on the number line.

   A: – 5   **B:** + 2   **C:** – 7   **D:** + 5   **E:** – 3

   b) How many spaces apart are the numbers?

   i) – 5 and – 4: _____   ii) – 2 and + 3: _____   iii) + 6 and + 8: _____

   c) How many negative numbers are greater than (ie. to the right of) – 4? _____

3. Leela recorded the winter temperatures shown in the chart.
   How much did the temperature change ...

   a) from Monday to Tuesday? _____

   b) from Tuesday to Wednesday? _____

   c) from Wednesday to Thursday? _____

Monday	Tuesday	Wednesday	Thursday
+ 5°C	– 2°C	– 7°C	+ 1°C

4. The chart shows the average temperature on the planets.

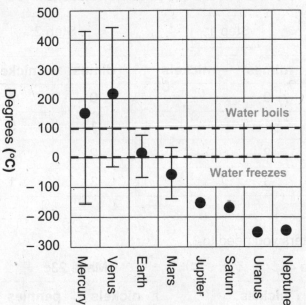

a) Which planet has the lowest temperature?

b) How much lower is the temperature on Uranus than on Jupiter?

c) The **range** of a set of numbers is the difference between the highest and lowest numbers.

   What is the range of temperatures on Mercury?

5. The number line below shows the approximate dates when animals were first domesticated.

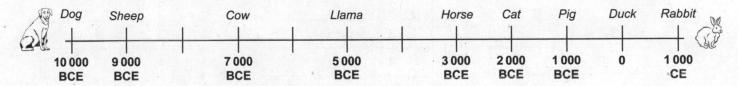

a) Which type of animal was domesticated first?

b) How many years after cows were domesticated were cats domesticated?

c) How many years after horses were domesticated were rabbits domesticated?

d) Pick two animals. How many years after the first animal was the second animal domesticated?

6. Mackerel live about 200 m below sea level.
   Gulper eels live at 1 000 m below sea level.
   Write integers for the depths where the animals live.
   How far below the mackerel does the gulper eel live?

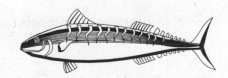

7. How many negative integers are greater than −6?

8. Why are −3 and +3 closer to each other than −4 and +4?

Many problems in mathematics and science have more than one solution.

If a problem involves two quantities, you can be sure you haven't missed any possible solutions if you list the values of one of the quantities in increasing order.

Example:

Find all the ways you can make 35¢ with dimes and nickels. Start with no dimes, then 1 dime, and so on up to 3 dimes (4 would be too many).

Then, count on by 5s to 35 to find out how many nickels you need to make 35¢.

Step 1:

dimes	nickels
0	
1	
2	
3	

Step 2:

dimes	nickels
0	7
1	5
2	3
3	1

---

1. Fill in the amount of pennies, nickels, dimes or quarters you need to…

a) Make 17¢

nickels	pennies
0	
1	
2	
3	

b) Make 45¢

dimes	nickels
0	
1	
2	
3	
4	

c) Make 23¢

nickels	pennies
0	
1	
2	
3	
4	

d) Make 32¢

dimes	pennies
0	
1	
2	
3	

e) Make 65¢

quarters	nickels
0	
1	
2	

f) Make 85¢

quarters	nickels

2.

quarters	nickels
0	
1	
2	

Ben wants to find all the ways he can make 60¢ using quarters and nickels. He lists the number of quarters in increasing order. Why did he stop at 2 quarters?

_____

_____

3. Make a chart to show all the ways you can make the given amount.

a) 90¢ using dimes and nickels

b) 125¢ using quarters and dimes

Example:

Alana wants to find all pairs of numbers that multiply to give 15.

There are no numbers that will multiply by 2 or 4 to give 15, so Alana leaves those rows in her chart blank.

The numbers in the last row of the chart are the same as those in the third row so Alana knows she has found all pairs.

$$1 \times 15 = 15 \qquad 3 \times 5 = 15$$

1st Number	2nd Number
1	15
2	---
3	5
4	---
5	3

----

4. Find all pairs of numbers that multiply to give the number in bold.

a) **6**

First Number	Second Number

b) **8**

First Number	Second Number

5.

quarters	dimes
0	
1	
2	

Alicia wants to find all the ways she can make 70¢ using quarters and dimes.

One of the entries on her chart won't work. Which one is it?

6. Find all the ways to make the amounts using quarters and dimes.
   NOTE: Some entries on your chart may not work.

a) 80¢

quarters	dimes
0	
1	
2	

b) 105¢

quarters	dimes

7. Find all the widths and lengths of a rectangle with perimeter 12 units.

Width	Length
1	

8. Make a chart to find all the pairs of numbers that multiply to give.

   a) 12   b) 14   c) 20   d) 24

Mass measures the amount of substance in a thing. **Grams** (g) and **kilograms** (kg) are units for measuring weight or mass.

One kilogram is equal to 1000 grams.

Things with a mass of about one **gram**:	Things with a mass of about one **kilogram**:
✓ A paper clip	✓ A one litre bottle of water
✓ A dime	✓ A bag of 200 nickels
✓ A chocolate chip	✓ A squirrel

One gram is equal to 1000 **milligrams** (mg): a milligram is 1000 times smaller than a gram. Milligrams are used to measure the mass of <u>very</u> small objects. A flea has a mass of about 10 mg.

---

1. What unit is more appropriate to measure each item? Circle the appropriate unit:

 grams or kilograms?   grams or kilograms?

 grams or kilograms?   grams or kilograms?

 grams or kilograms?   grams or kilograms?

2. Estimate the mass of the following things, in grams:

   a) a pen _____   b) an apple _____   c) this workbook _____

3. Can you name an object that has a mass of about one gram? _____

4. Estimate the mass of the following things in kilograms:

   a) your math book _____   b) your desk _____   c) a bicycle _____

5.

Penny	2.5 grams
Nickel	4 grams
Dime	2 grams
Quarter	4.5 grams
Loonie	7 grams

   a) What is the mass of…

      i) 75¢ in nickels?   ii) 15 dimes?

      iii) $2.00 in quarters?   iv) 200 loonies?

   b) How many quarters would have the same mass as 25 nickels? Explain.

   c) How many pennies would have the same mass as 6 nickels?

   d) Create a problem using the weights in the chart.

6.   What do you multiply a measurement in grams by to change it into milligrams? _____

7.   a)   Change the mass of both the loonie and nickel in Question 5 into milligrams:

   Nickel: _____   Loonie: _____

   b)   How many milligrams heavier than a nickel is a loonie? _____

8.   A monarch butterfly has a mass of about 500 mg.

   How many monarch butterflies would have a mass of about a gram? _____

   How many would have a mass of about a kilogram? _____

9.   Check off the appropriate box. Would you use milligrams, grams or kilograms to measure the mass of:

   a) a television?   ☐ mg ☐ g ☐ kg b) a grain of sand?   ☐ mg ☐ g ☐ kg

   c) a small beetle?   ☐ mg ☐ g ☐ kg d) a bed?   ☐ mg ☐ g ☐ kg

   e) a frog?   ☐ mg ☐ g ☐ kg f) an apple?   ☐ mg ☐ g ☐ kg

10. Write in the missing masses to balance the scales. The masses on the right hand scale are equal in each question:

   a)

   10 kg 10 kg 10 kg

   b)

   9 g 9 g

11. Solve the following word problems. Justify two of your answers.

   a)   The cost of shipping a package is $15.00 for each kilogram shipped.
        How much does it cost to ship a package that has a mass of 14 kilograms?

   b)   There are 35 mg of calcium in a vitamin pill.
        How many mg of calcium would you consume in a week if you had a vitamin pill every day?

   c)   A match box with matches has a mass of 20 g. The mass of the match box alone is 8 g.
        If there are 6 matches in the box, what is the mass of each match?

jump math
MULTIPLYING POTENTIAL.

Measurement 1

ME6-2: Volume

Volume is the amount of space taken up by a three dimensional object.

To measure volume, we can use 1 cm blocks. These blocks are uniform cubes, with length, width and height all 1 cm long:

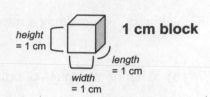

1 cm block
height = 1 cm
length = 1 cm
width = 1 cm

The volume of a container is based on how many of these 1 cm blocks will fit inside the container:

This object, made of centimetre cubes, has a volume of
4 cubes or 4 cubic centimetres (written 4 cm³).

----

1. Using "centicubes" as your unit of measurement, write the <u>volume</u> of each object:

   a)

   Volume = _____ cubes

   b)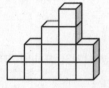

   Volume = _____ cubes

   c)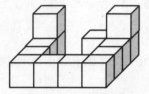

   Volume = _____ cubes

2. Given a structure made of cubes, you can draw a "mat plan" as shown:

3	1	2
1		

   ← The numbers tell you how many cubes are stacked in each position.

   For each figure below, fill in the missing numbers in the mat plan:

   a)

   b)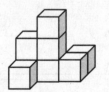

   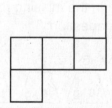

   c)

   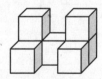

   d)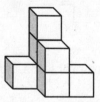

   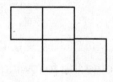

3. On grid paper, draw a mat plan for each of the following structures (use cubes to help):

   a)

   b)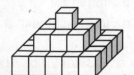

   c)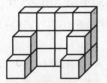

ME6-3: Volume of Rectangular Prisms

1. Use the number of blocks in the shaded column to write an addition statement and a multiplication statement for each area:

a) 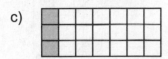 $3 + 3 + 3 + 3 = 12$
$3 \times 4 = 12$

b) 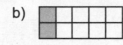   __ + __ + __ + __ + __ = ____

___ × ___ = _____

c)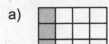

__ + __ + __ + __ + __ + __ + __ = ____

___ × ___ = _____

2. How many 1 cm³ blocks are in each shaded row? (Blocks are not shown to scale)

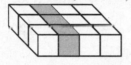   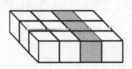   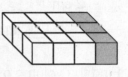

_____blocks   _____blocks   _____blocks   _____blocks

3. a) Write an addition statement for the volume of the shape:

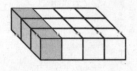   __ + __ + __ + __ = _____ cm³

b) Write a multiplication statement for the same volume: ___ × _4_ = _____ cm³

4.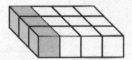

a) How many blocks are shaded? _____

b) Write an addition statement for the volume of the shape:

____ + ____ + ____ + ____ = _____ cm³

c) Write a multiplication statement for the same volume:

____ × 4 = _____ cm³

5. Write an addition and multiplication statement for each volume:

a)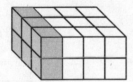

____ + ____ + ____ = _____ cm³

____ × _3_ = _____ cm³

b)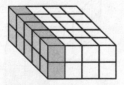

____ + ____ + ____ + ____ = _____ cm³

____ × ____ = _____ cm³

c)

____ + ____ + ____ + ____ + ____ = _____ cm³

____ × ____ = _____ cm³

6. Claire stacks blocks to make a tower.

   She finds the number of cubes in each tower by multiplying the number of cubes in the base by the number of layers.

   a)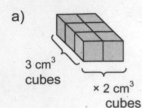

   3 cm³ cubes

   × 2 cm³ cubes

   2 cm³ × __3__

   = __6__ cm³

   b)

   blocks in each layer   number of layers

   2 cm³ × 3 × __2__

   = _____ cm³

   c)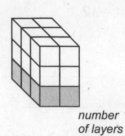

   number of layers

   2 cm³ × 3 × ____

   = _____ cm³

   d)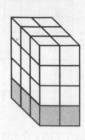

   2 cm³ × 3 × ____

   = _____ cm³

7. Find the volume of each prism.

   a)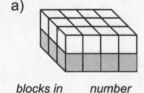

   blocks in each layer   number of layers

   _____ × _____

   = _____ cm³

   b)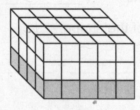

   _____ × _____

   = _____ cm³

   c)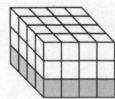

   _____ × _____

   = _____ cm³

   d)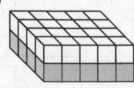

   _____ × _____

   = _____ cm³

8. Peter notices that the area of the base of a rectangular prism is the same number as the volume of the base layer of blocks.

   He calculates the volume of the prism by multiplying the area of the base layer by the number of layers. Will his method work for all rectangular prisms?

Area of base
6 cm²

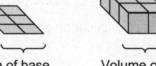

Volume of base
6 cm³

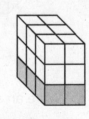

9.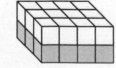

   A

   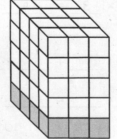

   B

   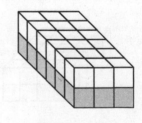

   C

   a) What is the area of the base of each structure?

   b) What is the volume of the base layer?

   c) What is the volume of the structure?

10. How many blocks are on the end of each prism?

a)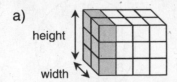

Number of blocks on end

= height × width

= __3__ × __2__ = __6__

b)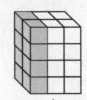

Number of blocks on end

= height × width

= _____ × _____ = _____

c)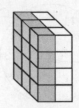

Number of blocks on end

= height × width

= _____ × _____ = _____

11. How many blocks are in each prism?

a)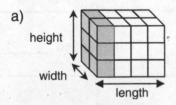

Number of blocks in prism

= height × width × length

= ___ × ___ × ___ = ___

b)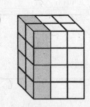

Number of blocks in prism

= height × width × length

= ___ × ___ × ___ = ___

c)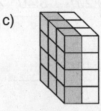

Number of blocks in prism

= height × width × length

= ___ × ___ × ___ = ___

12. Find the volume of each box with the indicated dimensions (assume all units are in metres):

    HINT: V = H × L × W

a)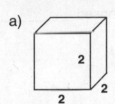

Width: _____

Length: _____

Height: _____

Volume = _____

b)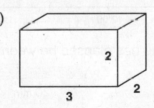

Width: _____

Length: _____

Height: _____

Volume = _____

c)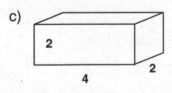

Width: _____

Length: _____

Height: _____

Volume = _____

d)

Width: _____

Length: _____

Height: _____

Volume = _____

13. Find the volumes of the rectangular prisms from the mat plans shown below:

a)

5	5	5
5	5	5

Width: _____

Length: _____

Height: _____

Volume = _____

b)

3	3
3	3

Width: _____

Length: _____

Height: _____

Volume = _____

c)

10	10	10	10	10
10	10	10	10	10

Width: _____

Length: _____

Height: _____

Volume = _____

1. By counting by 5s, find out how much time elapsed from...

a)

Start

Finish

5:10 to 5:30

_____

b)

4:10 to 4:40

_____

c)

11:20 to 11:55

_____

2. Count by 5s to show how much time has elapsed between ...

a) 8:45 and 9:20.   8:45 , 8:50 , _____, _____, _____, _____, _____, _____, _____
                      0   5   10   15

Time elapsed: _____

b) 3:40 and 4:10. _____, _____, _____, _____, _____, _____, _____, _____, _____

Time elapsed: _____

3. Find how much time has passed between the times in bold (intervals are not shown to scale).

a)

1:40 1:45 1:50 1:55 2:00   3:00   4:00 4:05

Time elapsed: _____

b) 10:50 10:55 11:00   12:00   1:00   2:00 2:05 2:10

Time elapsed: _____

4. Find out how much time has elapsed between ...

a) 9:40 and 12:10.

   Time elapsed: _____   [20 min] [ ] [ ] [ ]

   9:40 , 10:00 , 11:00 , 12:00 , 12:10

b) 6:55 and 11:20.

   Time elapsed: _____   [5 min] [ ] [ ] [ ] [ ] [ ]

   6:55 , 7:00 , _____, _____, _____, _____, 11:20

5. Find how much time has elapsed by subtracting the times.

   a)   3:43   b)   8:22   c) 11:48   d)   6:40   e)   3:42
        3:20   7:21   5:30   2:25   1:05
        ____   ____   ____   ____   ____

6. Draw a timeline to find out how much time has elapsed between ...

   a) 11:20 and 4:35.   b) 11:35 and 1:05.   c) 12:30 and 2:05.

7. Karl started studying at 7:25 and finished at 9:10. How long did he study?

ME6-5: Subtracting Times

Annie's train leaves at 4:48 p.m. It is now 2:53 p.m. To calculate her wait, Annie subtracts the times:

Step 1: 48 is less than 53, so Annie regroups 1 hour as 60 minutes.

```
   3   48 + 60            3   108            3   108
   4 : 48        →        4 : 48             4 : 48
 − 2 : 53              − 2 : 53            − 2 : 53
                                            1 : 55
```

Step 2: Annie completes the subtraction.

> She must wait for
> 1 hour and 55 minutes.

1. Regroup 1 hour as 60 minutes where necessary. Then complete the subtraction. The first one is started for you:

a)
```
   3   72
   4 : 12
 − 2 : 31
```

b)
```
  12 : 23
 − 8 : 51
```

c)
```
  10 : 38
 − 9 : 47
```

d)
```
   5 : 19
 − 4 : 29
```

e)
```
   6 : 26
 − 2 : 43
```

f)
```
   7 : 17
 − 1 : 56
```

g)
```
   8 : 12
 − 3 : 25
```

h)
```
   4 : 35
 − 2 : 48
```

i)
```
   3 : 41
 − 1 : 57
```

j)
```
   2 : 39
 − 1 : 23
```

k)
```
   7 : 23
 − 4 : 12
```

l)
```
   8 : 52
 − 6 : 35
```

m)
```
   9 : 15
 − 4 : 24
```

n)
```
  10 : 21
 − 5 : 48
```

o)
```
  11 : 00
 − 7 : 27
```

p)
```
  11 : 05
 − 4 : 38
```

Ray finds the difference in time between 10:25 a.m. and 4:32 p.m. as follows…

Step 1: He finds the difference between 10:15 a.m. and 12:00 noon.

Step 2: He adds 4 hours and 32 minutes to the result.

Step 3: He regroups 60 minutes as 1 hour.

```
                         11   60
  12 : 00      →         12 : 00            4 : 32          5 : 77  →  6 : 17
− 10 : 15              − 10 : 15          + 1 : 45
                          1 : 45            5 : 77
```

The difference is 6 hours and 17 minutes.

2. Using Ray's method, find the differences between the times given.

a) 10:20 a.m. and 4:35 p.m.

b) 6:52 a.m. and 8:21 p.m.

c) 2:38 a.m. and 9:45 p.m.

jump math
MULTIPLYING POTENTIAL

Measurement 1

1. Complete the following table using the pattern:

12-hr Clock	24-hr Clock
12:00 a.m.	00:00
1:00 a.m.	01:00
2:00 a.m.	02:00

12-hr Clock	24-hr Clock
9:00 a.m.	9:00
10:00 a.m.	
12:00 p.m.	12:00
1 p.m.	13:00

12-hr Clock	24-hr Clock
5:00 p.m.	17:00
6:00 p.m.	

2. What number must you add to 1 p.m. to change it to 24-hour clock notation? _____

   List 3 other times that change in the same way: _____

3. For each a.m./p.m. time, write the corresponding 24-hour clock notation:
   HINT: Only look at the chart above if you need help.

   a) 5:00 a.m. = _____   b) 11:00 p.m. = _____   c) 6:00 p.m. = _____

   d) 2:00 a.m. = _____   e) 3:00 p.m. = _____   f) 12:00 a.m. = _____

4. For each 24-hour clock notation, write the corresponding a.m./p.m. time.

   a) 07:00 = _____   b) 15:00 = _____   c) 13:00 = _____   d) 00:00 = _____

   e) 18:00 = _____   f) 17:00 = _____   g) 6:00 = _____   h) 23:00 = _____

5. Find the difference between the times:

   a) 23:00 and 9:45   b) 22:52 and 7:18   c) 17:51 and 14:02   d) 19:23 and 11:58

6. Complete the chart to show when David left each part of
   the museum (using 24-hour time).

	Start	Dinosaurs	Reptiles	Lunch	Ancient Egypt	Bat Cave
Time Spent		1hr 15 minutes	40 minutes	55 minutes	1 hr 25 minutes	5 minutes
Time Finished	10:30					

7. Describe any differences between the way time is written for a 24-hour and a 12-hour clock…

   a) …in the morning (a.m.)   b) …in the afternoon or evening (p.m.)

1. Fill in the charts.

a)

Days	Hours
1	24
2	
3	

b)

Weeks	Days
1	7
2	
3	

c)

Years	Weeks
1	52
2	
3	

d)

Years	Days
1	365
2	
3	

2. A decade is 10 years. A century is 100 years. Fill in the blanks.

a) 40 years = _____ decades

b) 60 years = _____ decades

c) 90 years = _____ decades

d) 200 years = _____ centuries

e) 800 years = _____ centuries

f) 1500 years = _____ centuries

g) 2 decades = _____ years

h) 3 centuries = _____ years

i) 40 decades = _____ centuries

3. Alexander Cartwright invented baseball in 1845.
About how many decades ago was this?

4. Guled waited in line for 140 minutes.
Amir waited for 2 hours 15 minutes. Who waited longer?

5. Tom worked for 2 hours 20 minutes. How long did Clara work if...

a) Tom worked 35 minutes longer than Clara?

b) Clara worked 45 minutes longer than Tom?

6. Boat B left the Halifax harbour one hour later than boat A.
Both boats traveled at a steady speed in the same direction.

Time	14:00	15:00	16:00	17:00	18:00	19:00	20:00
Distance from Harbour — Boat A	0 km	6 km					
Distance from Harbour — Boat B	0 km	0 km					40 km

a) How far apart were the boats at 17:00?
b) At what time did boat B catch boat A?

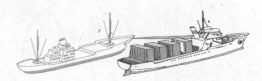

7. The Boeing 747 travels at a speed of about 14 km/minute.
Sound travels at a speed of about 344 m/second.
Which is faster?

BONUS
8. 1 mL of water drips from a tap every minute.
About how many L of water will leak from the tap in a year?

Venn diagrams are a way to use circles to show which objects have a property.

Objects inside a circle have the property and objects outside the circle do not.
NOTE: Polygons have straight sides.

 A B C D 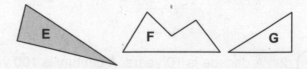 E F G

1. a) Which shape has both properties?
    Put its letter inside both circles.

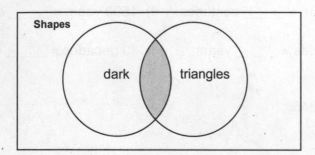

   b) Which shape has neither property?
    Put its letter outside both circles.

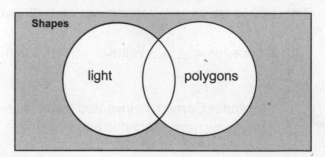

2. Complete the Venn diagrams.

   a)
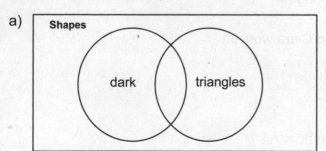

   b)
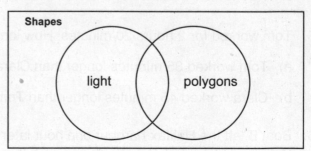

   c)

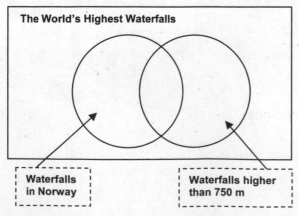

The World's Highest Waterfalls			
A	Angel	Venezuela	979 m
B	Tugela	South Africa	850 m
C	Utigord	Norway	800 m
D	Monge	Norway	774 m
E	Mutarazi	Zimbabwe	762 m
F	Yosemite	United States	739 m
G	Pieman	Australia	715 m
H	Espelands	Norway	703 m
I	Lower Mar Valley	Norway	655 m
J	Tyssestrengene	Norway	647 m

PDM6-2: Bar Graphs

A **bar graph** has 4 parts:

- a vertical and horizontal **axis**
- a **scale**
- **labels** (including a title)
- **data** (given by the bars)

The bars in a bar graph can either be vertical or horizontal. The scale tells how much each square on the axis represents. The labels indicate what the data in the bars is.

1.

Pets Owned by Students	Number of Students
Cat	12
Dog	15
Reptile	6
Bird	3
Other	10

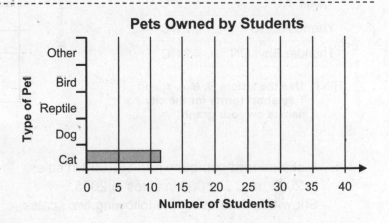

a) Complete the bar graph.

b) What scale was used in the bar graph? Do you think it was a good choice? Why or why not?

_____

c) Would you predict similar results for the students in your class? Explain.

_____

_____

2.

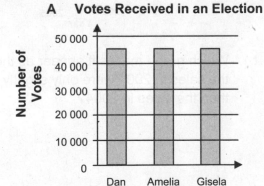

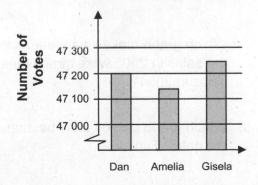

a) Find the scale on each bar graph.

b) Which graph makes it easier to tell the difference in votes for each candidate?

c) Who won the election?

Graph A: start at _____, count by _____, stop at _____.

Graph B: start at _____, count by _____, stop at _____.

3. Complete the bar graph to display the following data.

Recorded Temperatures by City (in °C)	
Brandon, MB	25°C
Medicine Hat, AB	27°C
Iqaluit, NU	12°C
Yarmouth, NS	21°C
Thunder Bay, ON	24°C

HINT: Use the letters B, M, I, Y, and T as short forms for the city names on your graph.

4. A skateboard company had $50 000 in sales in 2004, and $52 000 in sales in 2005. Show this data using the following two scales.

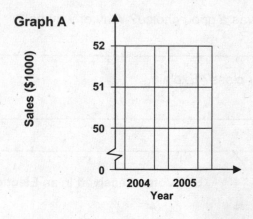

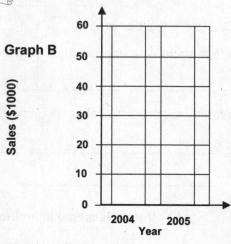

a) Which graph makes it appear as though the sales in 2005 were three times the sales in 2004?

b) Which graph makes it appear as though the sales in 2005 were only slightly more than the sales in 2004?

c) Which graph do you think best represents the data? Explain.

5. What scale would you use if you had to plot the following numbers? (Say what numbers the scale would stop and start at, and what size the intervals would be). Explain your choices.

a) 3, 2, 7, 9, 10
b) 14, 2, 16, 4, 8
c) 250, 1 000, 2 000
d) 12 000, 11 500, 12 500

PDM6-3: Double Bar Graphs

1. Two classrooms collected coats for charity from November to April.

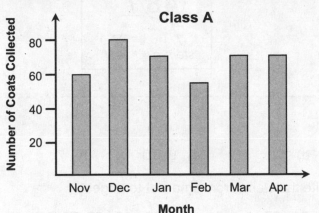

Class A

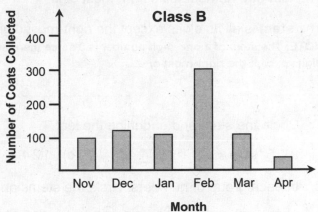

Class B

a) When you glance at the graphs, which class appears to have collected more coats? _____

Why? _____

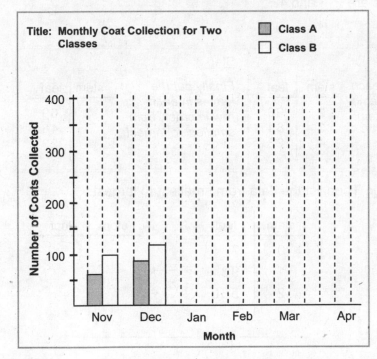

Title: Monthly Coat Collection for Two Classes

☐ Class A
☐ Class B

b) When you look closely at the scales, which class actually collected more? _____

c) Why are most of Class B's data so low on the graph?

_____

_____

_____

d) To compare the data, complete the graph on the left.

> A **double bar graph** compares two sets of data. The graph you drew in Question 1 d) is a double bar graph.

 e) In which month(s) did class A collect more coats than class B?

f) During one month in this period, Class B put an ad in a newspaper asking for coats. Which month do you think that was?

2. Draw a double bar graph using the data below. Include a title and labels.

	Favourite Sporting Activities			
	Baseball	Basketball	Tennis	Other
Girls	42	32	73	56
Boys	75	50	43	80

The **leaf** of a number is its right-most digit.

The **stem** is all its digits <u>except</u> the right-most digit.

NOTE: The stem of a one-digit number is 0 since there are no digits except the right-most one.

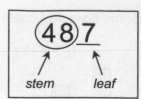

stem   leaf

---

1. Circle the stem and underline the leaf.

   a) <u>5</u> *stem is 0.*   b) ③<u>7</u>   c) 1 2 4   d) 5 1   e) 9 0 0 0   f) 7

2. In each group of numbers, circle the stems and write the stems from smallest to largest.

   a) ②3 9 8 ③4 ⑥5 ②8 ②5   b) 36 39 46 51 37 9 45   c) 107 88 87 75 104 96

   <u> 0 </u> <u> 2 </u> <u> 3 </u> <u> 6 </u>   <u>   </u> <u>   </u> <u>   </u> <u>   </u>   <u>   </u> <u>   </u> <u>   </u>

3. In the data set 38 29 26 42 43 34, the stems are 2, 3 and 4.
   To build a stem and leaf plot, follow these steps.

Step 1:			Step 2:			Step 3:		
Write the stems in order, from smallest to largest.	stem	leaf	*Then write each leaf in the same row as its stem:*	stem	leaf	*Finally put the leaves in each row in order, from smallest to largest.*	stem	leaf
	2			2	96		2	69
	3			3	84		3	48
	4			4	23		4	23

For each plot, put the leaves in the correct order. Then list the data from smallest to largest.

stem	leaf		stem	leaf
2	5 1		2	1 5
4	8 5 1	→	4	
5	6 2		5	

<u>21</u> <u>25</u> <u>   </u> <u>   </u> <u>   </u> <u>   </u>

stem	leaf		stem	leaf
0	7			
1	9 3	→		
2	5 8 0			

<u>   </u> <u>   </u> <u>   </u> <u>   </u> <u>   </u> <u>   </u>

4. Use the following data to create stem and leaf plots.

   a) 8 7 13 18 10   b) 99 97 103 99 101   c) 77 91 105 97 112 114 96 78

5. Stem and leaf plots make it easy to find the lowest and highest data values.

   i) Look for the smallest leaf in the first row to find the lowest data value.

   ii) Look for the largest leaf in the last row to find the highest data value.

   The **range** of a set of data is the difference between the lowest and the highest value.
   Find the range of the data sets in questions 3 and 4.

PDM6-5: Broken Line Graphs – An Introduction

A **broken line graph** has a horizontal and a vertical axis. Individual points are connected by a line.

1.

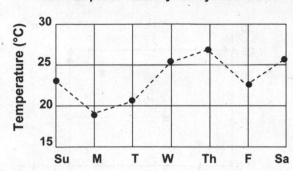

The Temperature in my Backyard this Week

a) What is the scale?

Start at _____, count by _____, stop at _____.

b) What is the title?

_____

c) What day was the coolest?

_____

d) What day was the warmest?

_____

e) What was the range of temperatures over the week?

_____

2.

Shoe Sales over the Past Year

a) In which month did the shoe store make the largest profit? The smallest profit?

b) How much profit did the shoe store make in January? In May?

c) In which months did the shoe store make more than $4000?

d) On which date do you think a star athlete signed shoes in the store?

February 1st   April 1st   July 1st   October 1st

Justify your answer.

The bar graph and the line graph below both show the price of CDs on sale.

Using a ruler, you could draw an arrow across from the '5 CD' bar to show 5 CDs cost $25.

Similarly you could draw a line up from the '5 CD' mark and then across to the $25 mark.

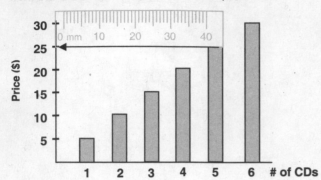
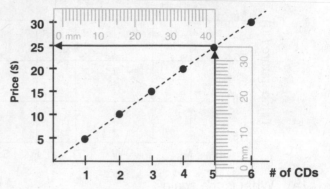

1. Draw arrows (using a ruler!) on the <u>line graph</u> above to find the cost of …

   a) 3 CDs: $ _____   b) 4 CDs: $ _____   c) 6 CDs: $ _____

2. To find out how many CDs you can buy for $20, you could draw arrows as shown.

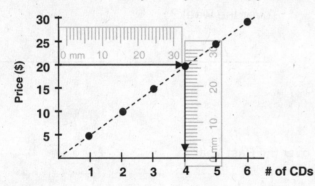

   Draw arrows (using a ruler!) on the line graph to find how many CDs you can buy for:

   a) $15: _____ CDs

   b) $25: _____ CDs

   c) $30: _____ CDs

3. These graphs show how much money Sally will earn painting houses in the summer.

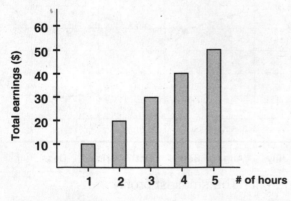
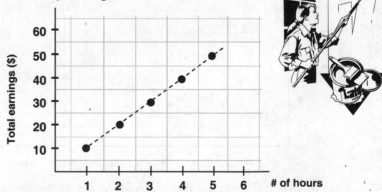

   a) On both graphs, show how much Sally would make for working: i) 3 hours   ii) 4 hours

   b) Draw arrows on the line graph to show how much Sally will earn in $3\frac{1}{2}$ hours.

   c) Extend the line graph to show how much Sally could make in: i) 6 hours   ii) $\frac{1}{2}$ hour

   d) Explain an advantage of a line graph over a bar graph.

A broken line graph is a good choice to display data if you want to predict what will happen outside the range of your data or between data points.

Answer the following questions in your notebook.

1. As the temperature rises, crickets chirp more frequently.

   About how many times would you predict the cricket would chirp at.

   a) 15°   b) 25°   c) 35°

   d) About how high would the temperature be if the cricket chirped 240 times a minute?

   Explain how you found your answer.

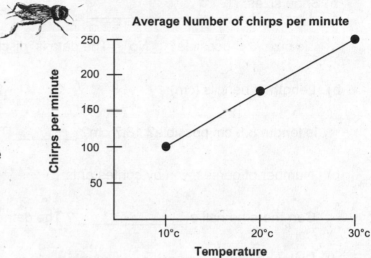

Average Number of chirps per minute

2. Would you use a broken line graph or a bar graph to display the data? Explain your choice of graph.

   a) Will next week's temperature be warmer or cooler?

Day	Su	M	T	W	Th	F	Sa
Temp (°C)	23	25	24	22	18	17	15

   b) Which city was warmest yesterday?

City	Toronto	Hamilton	Quebec	Montreal
Temp (°C)	27	24	19	25

   c) Will next year's profit be more or less than this year's?

Month	J	F	M	A	M	J	J	A	S	O	N	D
Profit ($1000)	3	2	3	3	4	4	5	5	5	6	6	7

3.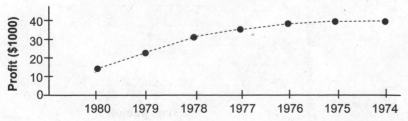

   Company's Earnings by Year

   a) Did the company's earnings increase or decrease over time?

   b) What did the company do to make it look like their earnings increased over time?

Data is **continuous** if all numbers between data values are possible. Otherwise, the data is **discrete**. Non-numerical data is always discrete.

----

1. Is the data discrete or continuous?

   a) Shoe sizes: 5   5   6 $6\frac{1}{2}$ 7   7   7   8 $8\frac{1}{2}$

   Is size $6\frac{1}{4}$ possible? __No__ The data is _discrete_ .

   b) Length of pencils (cm):   8   3   12   17.1   13.4   19   18.6

   Is length 8.5 cm possible? 18.7 cm? _____ The data is _____ .

   c) Number of games won by contestants: 7   6   8   12   4   0   3

   Can there be half a _____ ? The data is _____ .

   d) Distance Jenn runs each day (in km):   15   15   20   22   22   25

   Can there be half a _____ ? The data is _____ .

   e) Number of runners Jenn sees every day?   7   14   16   8   12   14

   Can there be half a _____ ? The data is _____ .

2. Decide whether the data on each axis is discrete or continuous. Explain your answer.

   a)

   b)

   c)

   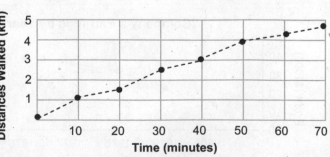

PDM6-9: Continuous Line Graphs

When data is continuous, you can use a **continuous line graph** to predict what happens in between data values.

1. How far from home was Katie after 10 minutes?

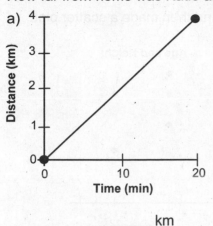

a)

_____ km

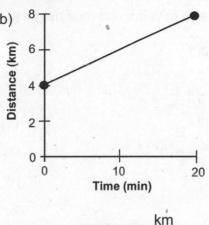

b)

_____ km

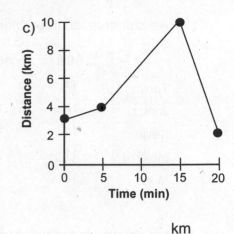

c)

_____ km

2. Draw a continuous line graph, then answer the question.

a) How much money did Tom earn for 3½ hours work?

Hours Worked	0	1	2	3	4
Money Earned ($)	0	10	20	30	40

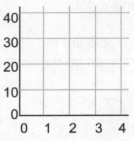

b) How far did Natalia walk in 2 ½ minutes?

Time (minutes)	0	1	2	3	4
Distance Walked (metres)	0	100	200	300	400

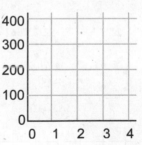

3. Sometimes graphs are drawn with solid lines (to show trends) even when data is not continuous.

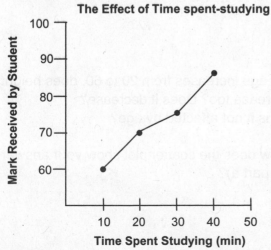

The Effect of Time spent-studying

a) Describe any trends you see in the graph.

b) Which data on the graph is not continuous? Explain.

c) Do you think the student would score over 90% if they studied for more than an hour?

Do you feel confident about your prediction? Explain and discuss with your peers.

Scatter Plots are used to show whether there is a relationship between two sets of data.
Each dot represents one set of data.

1. Five students recorded their age in years and their height in cm and then made a scatter plot.

	Age	Height
Tanya	11	150
Jomar	12	145
Kevin	11	160
Melanie	11	156
Mona	12	156

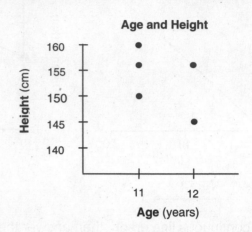

Each dot shows the height and age of one person.

a) Circle Melanie's dot.

b) Which two people are the same height?
   How is this shown on the scatter plot?

2.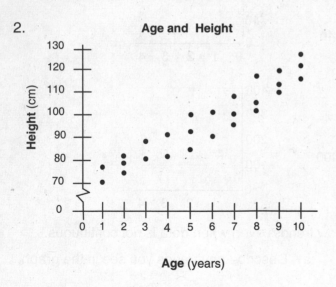

a) How many 5-year-olds are part of the data?

b) Were 10-year-olds on average taller or shorter

   than 9-year olds?

c) Was every 10-year-old taller than every 9-year-old?

d) As age increases from 1 to 10, does height tend to
   increase or decrease?

e) How does the scatter plot show this?

3.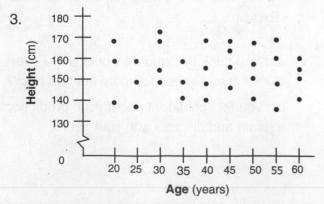

a) As age increases from 20 to 60, does height
   increase too? Does it decrease?
   Or is it not affected by age?

b) How does the scatter plot show your answer
   to part a)?

PDM6-11: The Mean

1. Move enough balls so that all rods have the same number of balls on each rod.
   The **mean** is the number of balls on each rod.

a)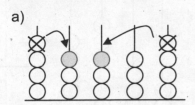

Mean: _____

b)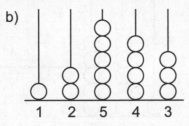

|1|2|5|4|3|

Mean: _____

c)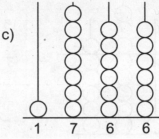

|1|7|6|6|

Mean: _____

2. Draw the number of balls given.
   Move balls to find the mean. (Shade the balls you moved.)

a)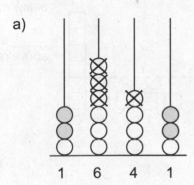

|1|6|4|1|

Mean: ____3____

b)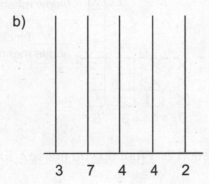

|3|7|4|4|2|

Mean: _____

c)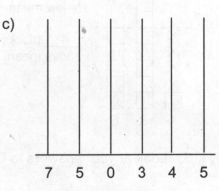

|7|5|0|3|4|5|

Mean: _____

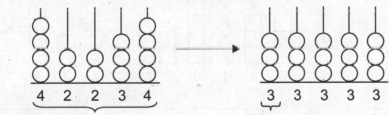

|4|2|2|3|4| → |3|3|3|3|3|

Number of balls = 4 + 2 + 2 + 3 + 4 = 15

Mean = Number of balls on each rod

= Total number of balls ÷ Number of rods

So **mean = sum of data values ÷ number of data values**.

3. Find the mean <u>without</u> using balls.

a) i) 0 3 4 6 7   ii) 1 4 5 7 8   iii) 2 5 6 8 9   iv) 3 6 7 9 10

☐ sum of data values

÷ ☐ number of data values

☐ mean

b) Explain how the mean changes when you add 1 to each data value.

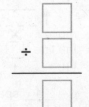

jump math
MULTIPLYING POTENTIAL.

Probability & Data Management 1

1. Find the mean and draw a horizontal line to show it.

a)
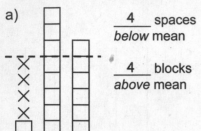

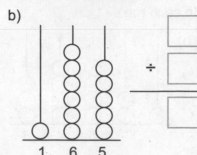

$$\div \begin{array}{c} 15 \\ 3 \\ \hline 5 \end{array}$$

1 8 6

b)
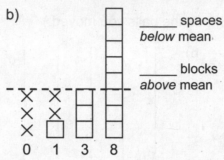

$$\div \square$$

1 6 5

c)
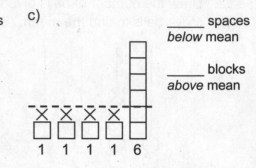

$$\div \square$$

2 3 6 5

2. Count the blocks above the mean and the spaces below the mean.

a)
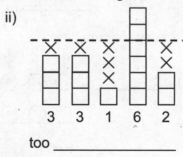

__4__ spaces *below* mean

__4__ blocks *above* mean

1 8 6

b)
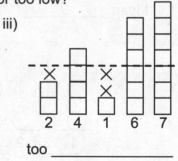

____ spaces *below* mean

____ blocks *above* mean

0 1 3 8

c)
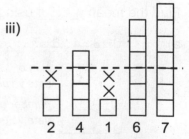

____ spaces *below* mean

____ blocks *above* mean

1 1 1 1 6

3. Look at your answers to Question 2. What do you notice? Explain.

4. Liana draws a line to guess where the mean is. Is her guess too high or too low?

a) i)

1 1 6 4

too ___low___

ii)

3 3 1 6 2

too _____

iii)

2 4 1 6 7

too _____

b) • If Liana's guess was *too low*, move the line up one.
    • If her guess was *too high*, move the line down one.
    • Then check to see if you have found the mean.

i)
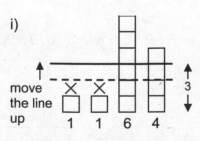

move the line up

1 1 6 4

__4__ spaces below the line.

__4__ blocks above the line.

The mean is __3__.

ii)
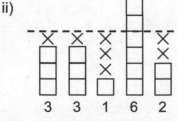

3 3 1 6 2

____ spaces below the line.

____ blocks above the line.

The mean is _____.

iii)
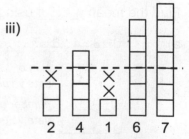

2 4 1 6 7

____ spaces below the line.

____ blocks above the line.

The mean is _____.

PDM6-13: Mean (Advanced)

1. The number of spaces below the mean is the same as the number of blocks above the mean.
   Write a number sentence to show this.

a)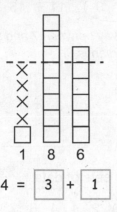

    1   8   6

    4 = ☐3☐ + ☐1☐

b)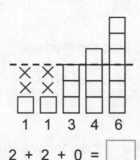

    1   1   3   4   6

    2 + 2 + 0 = ☐ + ☐

c)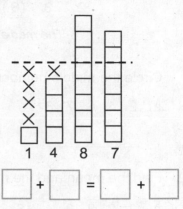

    1   4   8   7

    ☐ + ☐ = ☐ + ☐

 Complete the remaining parts of this question on grid paper. Draw the blocks and find the mean first.

d) 2   6   7   e) 3   4   8   6   9   f) 2   4   5   5

2. Find data sets with mean 4 using the number sentences. Draw balls to help you.

a)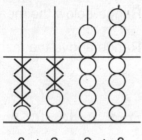

    3 + 2 = 2 + 3

Data: _1_ _2_ _6_ _7_

b)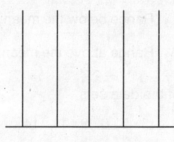

    2 + 2 + 1 = 2 + 3

Data: __ __ __ __ __

c)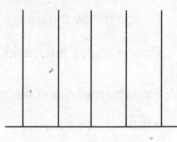

    1 + 1 + 1 + 1 = 4

Data: __ __ __ __

3. Daniel found some data about birds' eggs.

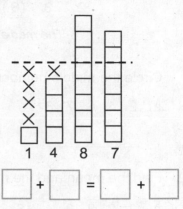

Bird	Clutch size	Egg length (cm)
Albatross	1	11
Emperor Penguin	1	12
Flamingo	1	9
Ostrich	9	14
Common Loon	2	9
White Storck	3	7
Ibis	3	6
Water Pheasant	4	4

2 m   *Ostrich*   50 cm   *Ibis*   110 cm   *Flamingo*

a) What is the mean length of the eggs?

b) What is the mean size of the clutches?

c) List the birds whose clutch size is below the mean.

d) Do the birds with smaller than average clutches have eggs shorter than the mean egg size?

e) Do the birds with the clutch size that is at least the mean size have smaller eggs?
   Which bird is exceptional?
   Why do you think this bird is exceptional?

Probability & Data Management 1

PDM6-14: The Median, Mean, and Range

1. To find the **median** of a data set, put the data in order. Count from either end until you reach the middle.

$\qquad$ 2 3 ⑥ 7 11 $\qquad\qquad\qquad$ 2 3 ⟨7 9⟩ 11 15

$\qquad$ The median is 6. $\qquad\qquad\qquad$ The median is half way between 7 and 9.
$\qquad\qquad\qquad\qquad\qquad\qquad\qquad\qquad$ The median is 8.

Circle the middle number or numbers. Find the median.

a) 2 4 6 7 8 $\qquad$ b) 2 3 3 8 $\qquad$ c) 7 9 13 14 26 $\qquad$ d) 3 4 6 10 11 17

_____ $\qquad$ _____ $\qquad$ _____ $\qquad$ _____

2. Find the mean and the median (and the ranges below and above) of the sets of data.

a) 2 2 3 3 4 16

Median: _____ Mean: _____

Range below the median: _____

Range above the median: _____

Range below the mean: _____

Range above the mean: _____

b) 1 16 15 2 21

Median: _____ Mean: _____

Range below the median: _____

Range above the median: _____

Range below the mean: _____

Range above the mean: _____

c) 2 1 4 6 7

Median: _____ Mean: _____

Range below the median: _____

Range above the median: _____

Range below the mean: _____

Range above the mean: _____

3. Find the mean and the median of the data sets.

a) 2 3 4 5 6

Median: _____ Mean: _____

b) 5 6 9 11 14

Median: _____ Mean: _____

c) 1 2 13 16 7 9

Median: _____ Mean: _____

Change one value in the set to make the mean larger than the median.

___ ___ ___ ___ ___ $\qquad$ ___ ___ ___ ___ ___ $\qquad$ ___ ___ ___ ___ ___ ___

Median: _____ Mean: _____ $\qquad$ Median: _____ Mean: _____ $\qquad$ Median: _____ Mean: _____

Change one value in the set to make the mean smaller than the median.

___ ___ ___ ___ ___ $\qquad$ ___ ___ ___ ___ ___ $\qquad$ ___ ___ ___ ___ ___ ___

Median: _____ Mean: _____ $\qquad$ Median: _____ Mean: _____ $\qquad$ Median: _____ Mean: _____

4. Describe the data in each set in Question 2. Is it spread out in the same way above and below the median?

5. Order the numbers in each set in Question 3 c). Draw a picture of block towers for each set. Mark the mean and the median.

PDM6-15: The Mode, Median, Mean, and Range

1. The class marks on a test were:

75	77	69	75	90	75	73	65	68	8
65	73	71	75	70	95	97	65	72	86

    a) Create a stem and leaf plot for the data.

    b) The **mode** of a data set is the value that occurs most often.
        Find the range, mode, median, and mean of the data.
        Which value is hardest to read from the stem and leaf plot? Explain.

    c) Describe the data. Is it spread out more...
        i)   above or below the mean?   ii) above or below the median?

    d) Tom's mark was 75.
        Which of the following statements that he told his parents were true?
        Explain using mean, mode, median or range.

        i)   I did better than half of the class!

        ii)   My grade is higher than the average!

        iii) A lot of students had the same grade as me.

        iv)   Only 6 students did better than me!

        v)   75 is the most common mark.

        What do you think of Tom's mark? Discuss.

2. Can you add one positive number to the set 12, 14, 16 so that the new set has ...

Median:	10?	13?	14?	15?	20?
Mean:	10?	14?	20?		
Mode:	10?	12?	14?	20?	

3. Ron counted the number of floors of the buildings in his block:

    5, 3, 3, 1, 13

    a) Find the mean, median and modes of the set of data.

    b) The five story building is replaced by a skyscraper of 50 floors.

        Find the mean, median and the mode of the new data set.

    c) The number 50 is much greater than others. (It is called **an outlier**).

        Which value changed the most when you added the outlier, the mean, or the median?

4. Find a set of data, not all values equal, so that the range below the median is 0.
    Find the mean and the mode.

Answer the following questions in your notebook.

1.

Test #	1	2	3	4	5	6	7	8	9	10	11	12
Score	68	73	75	82	78	75	78	78	83	86	93	91

a) Draw a stem and leaf plot and a broken line graph for Sonya's math scores.

b) Answer the following questions and say which graph you used to find the answer.

   i) On how many tests did she score between 78 and 88?

   ii) What mark did she score most often?

   iii) Did her mark tend to increase or decrease throughout the year?

   iv) After which tests did her mark decrease?

   v) What was her highest score?

2.

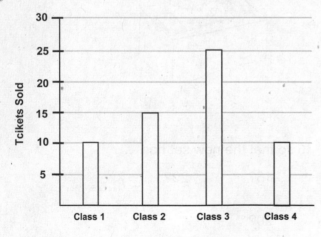

Concert Ticket Sales in Katia's Grade

a) How many tickets did Katia's grade sell altogether?

b) On average, how many tickets did each class sell?

c) $\frac{2}{3}$ of the tickets sold were adult tickets.

   How many adult tickets were sold?

d) Adult tickets sell for $5.00 and children's tickets sell for $2.00.
   Calculate the total value of the tickets sold.

e) The money from the school concert is going toward a grade-wide trip. The trip costs $300.
   i) How much more money is needed?
   ii) How many adult tickets would have to be sold to cover the remaining cost?

3. Match each type of graph with its purpose. The first one has been done for you.

Line Graph ——————————— Compares two sets of data.

Stem and Leaf Plot ——— Shows a trend in data or makes predictions (usually used when graphing change over time).

Double Bar Graph   Shows the frequency of results and trends clearly.

Bar Graph   Shows whether one type of data increases, decreases or neither when another type of data increases.

Scatter Plot   Makes it easy to see the largest, smallest and most common data values.

4. Choose and draw an appropriate type of graph to represent each set of data. Explain your choice.

a) Age and monthly allowance of different people.

Age	10	12	11	8	12	9	8	10	13	13	9	12	11	8	13
Monthly Allowance ($)	40	80	50	10	100	75	20	30	60	70	30	20	60	30	90

b) Thickness of rulers produced by a company (in tenths of a mm).

28 29 31 30 28 27 24 31 31 30 31 30 29 29 28 26 32 33 30 28

5. Which scatter plot best represents the relationship between height of people and their shoe size? Explain.

a)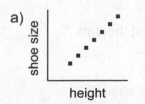

b)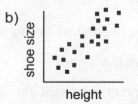

c)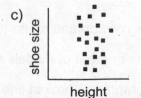

d)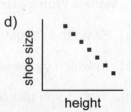

6.

| Average Monthly Rainfall or Precipitation (in cm) | | | |
Coniferous Forests	Tundra	Grasslands	Rainforest
January — 25	10	100	120
February — 20	10	100	120
March — 25	10	100	120
April — 35	10	20	120
May — 45	13	10	120
June — 50	18	5	120
July — 60	18	5	120
August — 55	13	5	120
September — 50	10	10	120
October — 40	10	20	120
November — 40	10	60	120
December — 35	5	100	120
Graph —			

a) Which graph best matches the data in each column? Write the letter of the correct graph under each column.

A 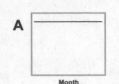   B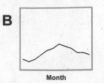

C 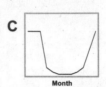   D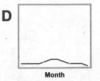

b) Describe any trends you see in the graphs. How do you account for the trends?

c) Sketch a graph that you think would represent the average monthly temperature where you live.

7.
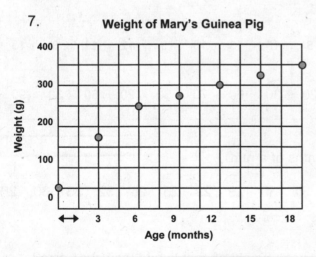

Weight of Mary's Guinea Pig

a) How many months does the interval shown by the arrow represent?

b) How many weeks does the interval represent?

c) Describe the trend you see in the graph.

d) The guinea pig was born at the beginning of January. In which month did it weigh 250 g?

e) Between which months did it grow the fastest?

8.

Year	1964	1968	1972	1980	1984	1988	1992	1996	2000	2004
Number of Olympic Medals Won by Brazil	1	3	2	4	8	9	3	15	12	10

a) State the range, mode, median and mean (to the nearest whole number) of the data.

b) In which years were the number of medals above the mean?

c) Would you use a bar graph or a broken line graph to represent the data? Explain.

> Data you collect yourself is called **primary (or first-hand) data.**

1. How would you collect primary data to answer each question?

   S. survey   **O.** observation   **M.** measurement

   a) Are more people born in the winter or summer?

   b) Does it take longer to run 5 km or to walk 1 km?

   c) What fraction of bikers wears helmets?

   d) What are your friends favourite books?

   e) How many birds visit the school yard each day?

> Data collected by someone else (that you find in sources like books or the internet) is called **secondary (or second-hand) data.**

2. Would you use **A.** primary   OR   **B.** secondary data to find out…

   a) …how long it takes for each member of your family to run 100 metres?

   b) Which baseball player has the most home runs?

   c) …the world record for the most number of sit-ups in a minute?

   d) …the average number of words you can write in a minute?

   e) What is the average age of maple trees in Quebec?

3. Make up a question that you would answer using

   a) first-hand data.

   b) second-hand data.

1.

> In written English, the letter "E" occurs more often than any other letter. The average number of times a letter such as "e" appears in a person's writing (and the average length of words and sentences) is different for every person. Detectives solving crimes can use these differences to decide who wrote a given text. And code breakers can use the average frequency of letters to break secret codes.

CD(E)FG

	In First Word	In First Sentence	In Whole Paragraph
# of e's	0	11	63
Total # of Letters	2	59	321

a) About what fraction of the letters are "e"? (Change to a decimal and round to the leading digit.)

In the first word

$\frac{0}{2}$ = 0

In the first sentence

In the paragraph

b) Can you estimate what fraction of letters are "e" from looking at the first word? Explain.

c) Does looking at the first sentence give a better estimate? Explain.

d) In English text, about 13 out of every 100 letters are "e".
Does the above paragraph have a higher or lower than average number of e's?

2. Explain who you would survey if you wanted to know…

a) how many people in Canada use outdoor skating rinks:

    A. all Canadians   or   **B.** only a sample?

b) how many people from your hockey team will show up for the next game:

    A. every player on the team   or   **B.** only a sample?

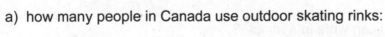

3. You want to know what equipment to put in a playground.
Would you survey only three- to eight-year-olds?
Justify your answer.

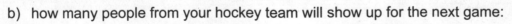

1. A school principal wants school to start and end half an hour earlier.
   To find out what students think, she does two surveys.

   A: She asks the first 50 students who arrive in the morning.   YES   40   NO   10

   B: She asks 5 students from each of the ten classrooms.   YES   20   NO   30

   a) Why didn't the two surveys produce the same results?

   b) Which group's opinion will be most similar to the whole school's opinion?

   c) There are 500 students in the school.
   About how many do you think will want school to start and finish half an hour earlier? Explain.

> A **representative sample** is similar to the whole population.
> A **biased sample** is not similar to the whole population because
> some part of the population is not represented.

2. Which sample is representative and which is not? Explain.

   a) A school is planning a party. To find out which songs are most popular, students ask:

   A: 40 grade 6 students
   B: 5 students from each grade

   b) A class wants to compare the heart rate of children before and after
   30 minutes of exercise. They take the heart rate of:

   A: 30 members of the school basketball teams
   B: 30 students selected at random from the school

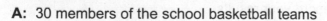

3. A city wants to build a new library, a new amusement park or a new baseball stadium.
   Explain how a survey given at each location would be biased.

   A: a professional baseball game

   B: a bookstore

   C: a professional hockey game

   D: a hip-hop concert

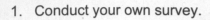

1. Conduct your own survey.

   Record all of your ideas, data, observation and conclusions.

   a) Decide what you want to learn.

   b) Decide how to ask your questions. What answers do you expect?

   c) Who should you survey? Is the sample representative or biased?
      Are you including enough people to give an accurate answer?

   d) Create a table to keep track of the responses you'll get. For example:

How do you get to school?	Tally
Walk	
Take the bus	
Ride my bike	

2. Design your own experiment.

   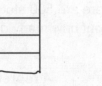

   a) Decide on your question.

   Examples:
   • How does adding salt to ice affect how fast it melts.
   • Do tomato seeds grow more quickly in direct sun or shade?

   b) What do you need to measure?

   c) How will you measure your results? What materials and equipment will you need?

   d) How will you make sure your experiment gives reliable results?
      You will need to keep everything except what you want to measure constant.

   e) Draw the table you will use to record your results.

   For both your survey and your experiment you will need to:
   • Choose and draw an appropriate type of graph to display your data.
   • Summarize your conclusions.

   BONUS
   Can you explain the results of your survey and experiment?

All polygons have sides (or 'edges') and vertices (the 'corners' where the edges meet).

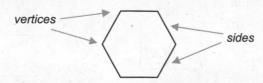

vertices   sides

NOTE: A polygon is a 2-D (flat) shape with sides made of straight lines.

HINT:
To avoid missing sides and vertices when you count, you should ...

mark the sides and circle the vertices.

---

1. Find the number of sides and vertices in each of the following figures.
    HINT: Mark the sides and circle the vertices as you count.

a)

____ sides ____ vertices

b)

____ sides ____ vertices

c)

____ sides ____ vertices

d)

____ sides ____ vertices

e)

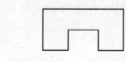

____ sides ____ vertices

f)

____ sides ____ vertices

2. Peter names the shapes according to how many sides they have.

a)

___ sides

triangle

b)

___ sides

quadrilateral

c)

___ sides

pentagon

d)

___ sides

hexagon

3. Complete the chart. Find as many shapes as you can for each shape name.

     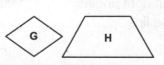

Shapes	Letters
Triangles	
Quadrilaterals	

Shapes	Letters
Pentagons	
Hexagons	

 4. On grid paper, draw a polygon with: a) 4 sides   b) 6 sides

5. How many sides do three quadrilaterals and five pentagons have altogether?
    How did you find your answer?

G6-2: Introduction to Angles

TEACHER: Before starting this worksheet, review right angles with your class.

1. Mark each angle as (i) a **right angle**; (ii) **less than** a right angle; OR (iii) **greater than** a right angle.
   Check your answers with the corner of a piece of paper.

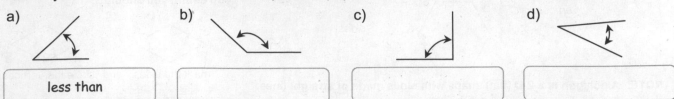

a)   less than

b)

c)

d)

2. Mark all the right angles in the following figures. Then circle the figures that have <u>two</u> right angles.

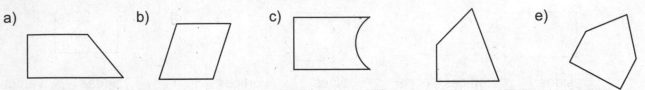

a)   b)   c)   e)

3. Mark any right angles in the shapes below with a square.   Mark any angles less than a right angle with a single line.   Mark any angles greater than a right angle with a double line.

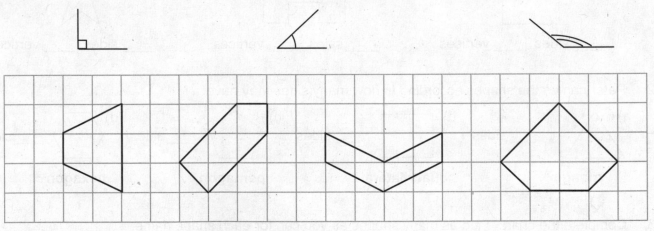

4. Mark all half right angles with a single line.   Mark any angle less than a half right angle with a dot.   Mark any angle greater than a half right angle and less than a right angle with a check.

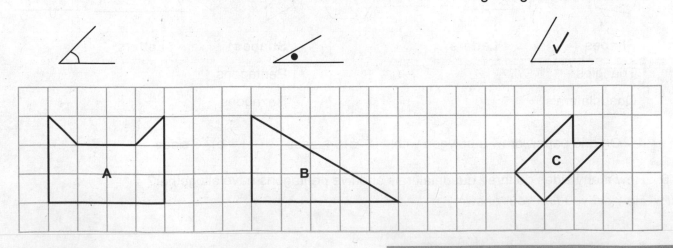

G6-3: Measuring Angles

To measure an angle, you use a **protractor**. A protractor has 180 subdivisions around its circumference. The subdivisions are called degrees. 45° is a short form for "forty-five degrees."

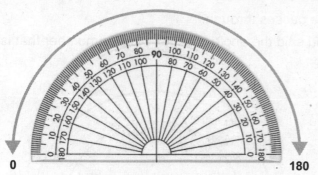

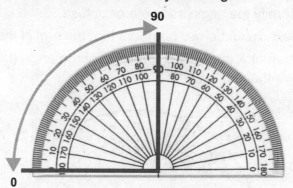

There are 180 subdivisions (180°) around the outside of a protractor.

There are 90° in a right angle (or a square corner).

Angles that are *less* than 90° are called **acute** angles.

Angles that are *more* than 90° are called **obtuse** angles.

---

1. Without using a protractor, identify each angle as <u>acute</u> or <u>obtuse</u>.

a)

b)

c)

d)

e)

f)
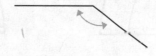

g)

h)
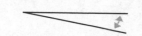

i)

G6-3: Measuring Angles (continued)

A protractor has two scales. The exercise below will help you decide which scale to use.

2. Identify the angle as acute or obtuse.

   Next circle the *two* numbers that the arm of the angle passes through.

   Then pick the correct measure of the angle (i.e. if you said the angle is acute, pick the number that is less than 90°).

a)

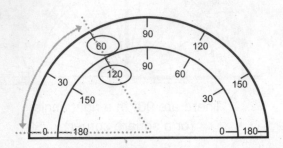

The angle is: _____acute_____

The angle is: _____60°_____

b)

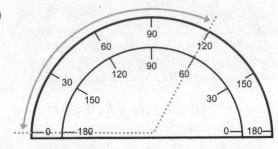

The angle is: _____

The angle is: _____

c)

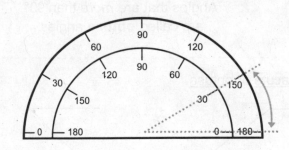

The angle is: _____

The angle is: _____

d)

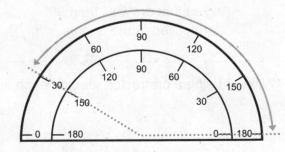

The angle is: _____

The angle is: _____

3. Again, identify the angle as acute or obtuse. Then measure the angle.

a)

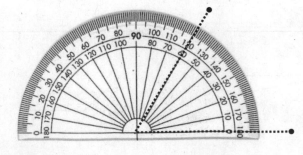

_____

b)

_____

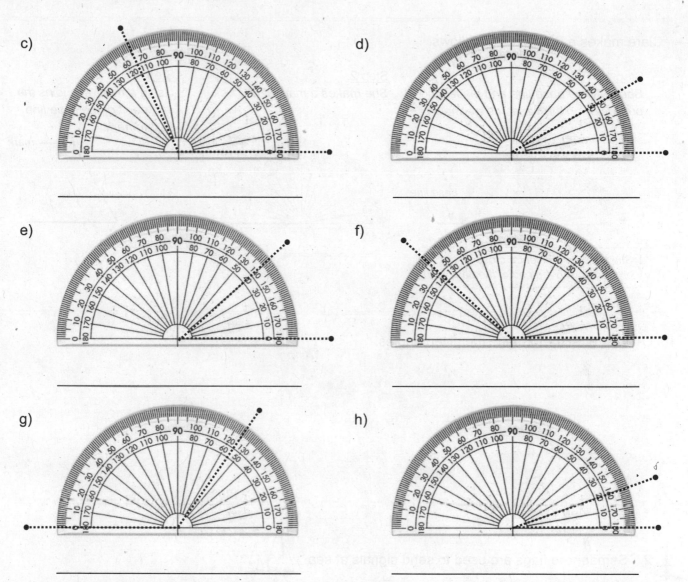

c)

_____

d)

_____

e)

_____

f)

_____

g)

_____

h)

_____

4. Measure the angles using a protractor. Write your answers in the boxes provided – don't forget units!
   HINT: For one question, you will have to turn the page (or the protractor!) upside down.

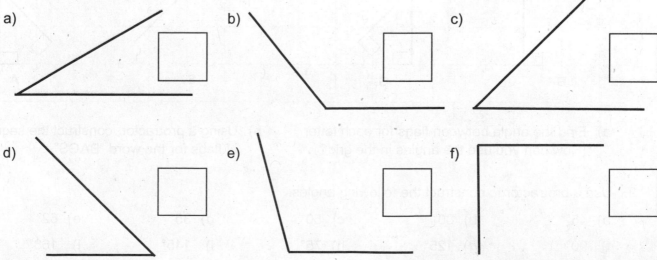

a)

b)

c)

d)

e)

f)

G6-4: Constructing Angles

Clare makes a 60° angle as follows:

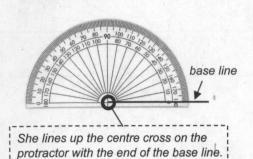

Step 1:
She draws a base line and places the protractor on the base line as shown.

base line

She lines up the centre cross on the protractor with the end of the base line.

Step 2:
She makes a mark at 60°.

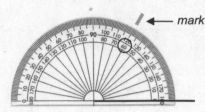

← *mark*

Step 3:
Using a ruler, she joins the end point of the base line to her mark.

← *mark*

1. Use a protractor to make the given angles.

     30°   120°

2. Semaphore flags are used to send signals at sea.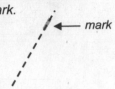

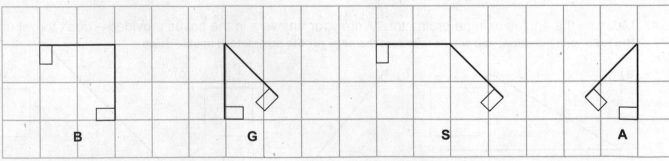

B   G   S   A

a) Find the angle between flags for each letter. (How can you use the angles in the grid?)

b) Using a protractor, construct the sequence of flags for the word "BAGS".

3. Use a protractor to construct the following angles.

a) 45°   b) 80°   c) 50°   d) 35°   e) 62°

f) 90°   g) 125°   h) 75°   i) 145°   j) 168°

G6-5: Angles in Triangles and Polygons

RECALL: An <u>acute</u> angle is less than 90°, an <u>obtuse</u> angle is greater than 90° and a <u>right</u> angle is exactly 90°.

Triangles can be classified by the size of their angles.

(i)   An **acute-angled triangle** has all acute angles.

(ii) An **obtuse-angled triangle** has an obtuse angle.

(iii) A **right-angled triangle** has a 90° angle.

If you measure the angles in a triangle accurately, you will find that they always add up to 180°.

----

1. Classify each triangle as <u>acute</u>, <u>obtuse</u> or <u>right-angled</u>.

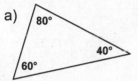 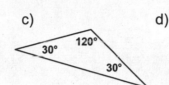 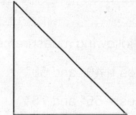 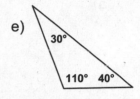

a) 80° 40° 60°   b) 45° 90° 45°   c) 30° 120° 30°   d) 40° 70° 70°   e) 30° 110° 40°

_____ _____ _____ _____ _____

2. Measure all of the angles in each triangle and write your measurement in the triangle. Then say what type of triangle it is.

a)   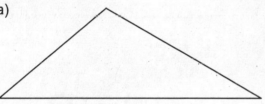   b) 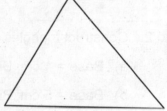   c)

_____   _____   _____

3. Measure all the angles in each shape (write your answers in the polygons). Then use the Venn diagram to classify the shapes.

a) A   b) B   c) C

  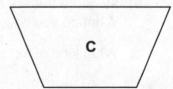

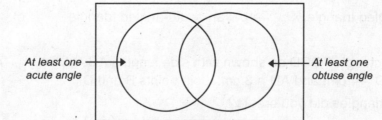

At least one ⟶ acute angle   ⟵ At least one obtuse angle

What is the name of the shape above that has all obtuse angles? _____

G6-6: Constructing Triangles and Polygons

1. You can construct a triangle, starting from a given base line (or base), by following these steps.

   (i) Using a protractor, construct an angle at each end of the base:

   (ii) Extend the arms of your angles until they meet:

   Following these steps, construct triangles using the bases given below. Make sure the base angles of your triangles are equal to the angles written on each end of the base.

   a)

   b)

   30°   60°   40°   90°

2. Construct triangles with the following measurements:

   a) Base = 4 cm; Base angles = 40° and 50°

   b) Base = 5 cm; Base angles = 55° and 75°

   c) Sides = 5 cm and 8 cm; Angle between these two sides = 25°

3. a) Construct three triangles with a 5 cm base and having base angles.

   (i) 30° and 30°   (ii) 60° and 60°   (iii) 45° and 45°

   b) Measure the sides of the triangles you drew.
      What do you notice about the lengths of the sides?

   c) What kind of triangles did you draw?

4. Draw free hand sketches of ...

   a) a right-angled triangle   b) an acute-angled triangle   c) an obtuse-angled triangle

5. Construct a rectangle ABCD as shown with side lengths AB = 4 cm, BC = 3 cm, CD = 4 cm, and AD = 3 cm. Join points B and D. What kind of triangles did you create?

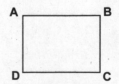

6. A rhombus is a four-sided figure with equal sides. Construct a rhombus with sides of 6 cm, and base angles of 60° and 120°.

G6-7: Naming Angles

To name an angle, follow these steps.

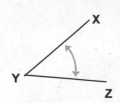

(i)   Write an angle sign, i.e. ∠

(ii) Write the letter of a point that lies on one of the arms of the angle, i.e. ∠X̲ (or ∠Z̲)

(iii) Write the letter of the vertex that lies at the centre of the angle, i.e. ∠XY̲ (or ∠ZY̲)

(iv) Write the letter of the point on the other arm of the angle, i.e. ∠XYZ̲ (or ∠ZYX̲)

---

1. In each triangle mark ∠ABC. Then measure the angle.

a)
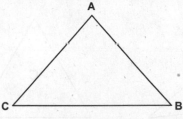

b)

c)
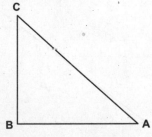

Measure of ∠ABC: _____   Measure of ∠ABC: _____   Measure of ∠ABC: _____

2. In each polygon mark angle ∠XYZ. Then measure the angle.

a)
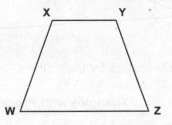

b)
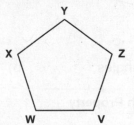

c)
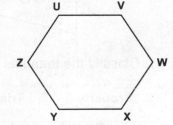

Measure of ∠XYZ: _____   Measure of ∠XYZ: _____   Measure of ∠XYZ: _____

3.
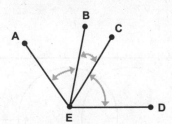

Name each of the angles marked. Then measure the angles.

measure of _____ = _____

measure of _____ = _____

measure of _____ = _____

Write the angles in order from least to greatest: _____

4.
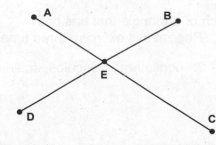

Write the names of two acute angles and two obtuse angles.

acute angles: _____ _____

obtuse angles: _____ _____

G6-8: Classifying Triangles

Triangles can be classified by the size of their angles, but they can also be classified by the length of their sides.

(i)   In an **equilateral triangle**, all three sides are of equal length.

(ii) In an **isosceles triangle**, two sides are of equal length.

(iii) In a **scalene triangle**, no two sides are of equal length.

---

1. Measure the <u>angles</u> and <u>sides</u> (in cm – or mm if necessary) of each triangle, and write your measurements on the triangles. Then use the charts to classify the triangles.

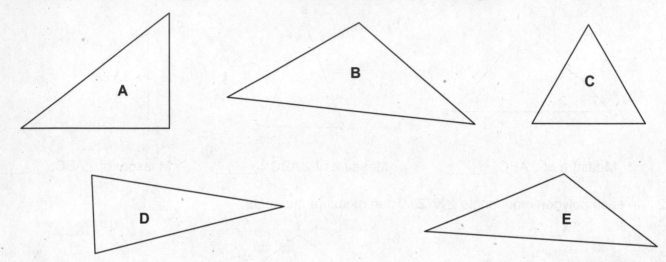

a) Classify the triangles by their angles.

Property	Triangles with Property
Acute-angled	
Obtuse-angled	
Right-angled	

b) Classify the triangles by their sides.

Property	Triangles with Property
Equilateral	
Isosceles	
Scalene	

2. Sort the triangles in Question 1 by their properties.

a)

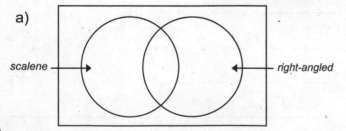

scalene →   ← right-angled

b)

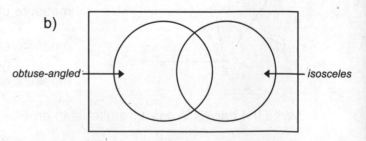

obtuse-angled →   ← isosceles

3. Pick one property from each list below and draw a rough sketch of a triangle that has both properties. If you can't sketch the triangle, write "impossible". (Repeat this exercise three times.)

List 1: acute-angled, obtuse-angled, right-angled   **List 2:** equilateral, isosceles, scalene

G6-9: Triangles

1. On the dot paper, draw ...

   a) An isosceles triangle with one right angle   b) An obtuse isosceles triangle

2. Each triangle below has two names, one in List 1 and one in List 2.

   List 1: acute-angled, obtuse-angled, right-angled

   List 2: equilateral, isosceles, scalene

   Measure the angles and sides in the triangles, then fill in their correct names.

   a)
   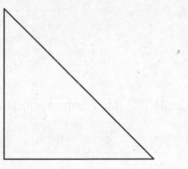

   b)
   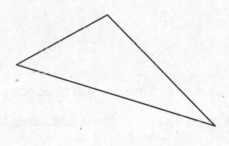

   Name from **List 1:** _____   Name from **List 1:** _____

   Name from **List 2:** _____   Name from **List 2:** _____

3. ➤ In an isosceles triangle, the two base angles (marked with an **x** in △ABC) are always equal.

   ➤ The angles in a triangle always add up to 180°.

   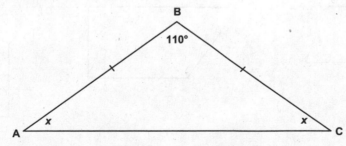

   How can you use the information given above to find the value of **x**?

   _____

   _____

G6-10: Parallel Lines

Parallel lines are like railway tracks (on a straight section of track) – that is, they are:

✓ Straight

✓ Always the same distance apart

No matter how long they are, parallel lines will <u>never</u> meet.

NOTE:
Lines of different lengths can still be parallel (as long as they are both straight and are always the same distance apart).

NOTE:
Mathematicians use arrows to indicate that certain lines are parallel:

These two lines are parallel

---

1. Mark any pairs of lines that are parallel with arrows (see note above).

a)

b)
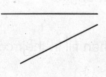

c)

d)

BONUS

e) Select one of the pairs of lines above that <u>are not</u> parallel. Put the corresponding letter here: ____

How do you know these lines aren't parallel?

2. Each of the shapes below has **one pair** of parallel sides. Put an 'X' through the opposite sides that <u>are not</u> parallel. The first one has been done for you.

a)

b)

c)

d)

e)

f)

g)

G6-10: Parallel Lines *(continued)*

NOTE:

If a figure contains <u>more than a single pair</u> of parallel lines, you can avoid confusion by using a different number of arrows on each pair:

Example: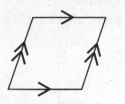

3. Using arrows, mark any pairs of parallel lines in the figures below.
   NOTE: One figure has three pairs of parallel lines – you will need three different sets of arrows.

a) 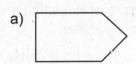   b)    c)    d)

_____ pairs   _____ pairs   _____ pairs   _____ pairs

e)   f)    g)   h)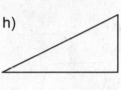

_____ pairs   _____ pairs   _____ pairs   _____ pairs

4. Each figure below has a set of three sides that are all parallel. Mark all three sides with arrows.

a) 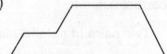   b) 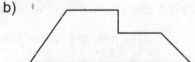   c)

5. On the grid, draw ...

   a) ... a pair of horizontal lines that are parallel and two units apart

   b) ... a pair of vertical lines that are parallel and that have different lengths

   c) ... a figure with one pair of parallel sides

6. Mark any parallel line segments in each letter.

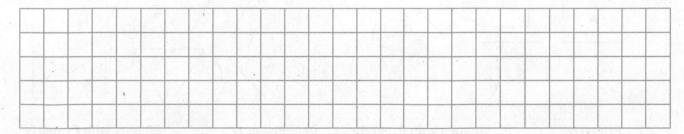

a) E   b) H   c) M   d) W   e) K

Some quadrilaterals have *no* pairs of parallel lines. Some have *one* pair of parallel lines. **Parallelograms** have *two* pairs of parallel lines.

 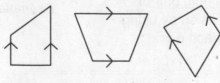 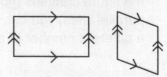

NO *pairs of parallel lines*   **ONE** *pair of parallel lines*   **TWO** *pairs of parallel lines*

---

1. For each of the shapes below, mark the parallel lines with arrows. Mark any pairs of sides that are not parallel with X's. Under each quadrilateral, write how many <u>pairs</u> of sides are parallel.

 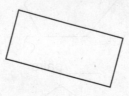 

A _____   B _____   C _____   D _____

 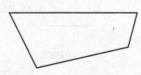 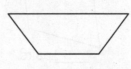

E _____   F _____   G _____   H _____

2. Sort the shapes **A** through **H** into the chart by writing the letter in the correct column.

No pairs of parallel sides	One pair of parallel sides	Two pairs of parallel sides

3. Using the figures below, complete the two charts. Start by marking the right angles and parallel lines in each figure.

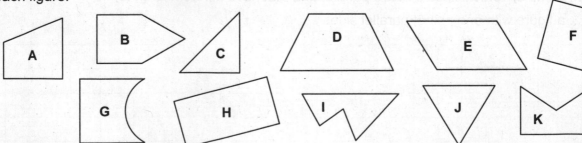

a)

Property	Shapes with Property
No right angles	
1 right angle	
2 right angles	
4 right angles	

b)

Property	Shapes with Property
No parallel lines	
1 pair	
2 pairs	

G6-11: Properties of Shapes *(continued)*

4. Using your ruler, measure the sides of the shapes below. Circle those that are equilateral.

   NOTE: A shape with all sides the same length is called <u>equilateral</u>. ("Equi" comes from a Latin word meaning "equal" and "lateral" means "sides".)

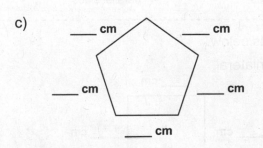

a) ____ cm   ____ cm   ____ cm   ____ cm

b) ____ cm   ____ cm   ____ cm   ____ cm

c) ____ cm   ____ cm   ____ cm   ____ cm   ____ cm

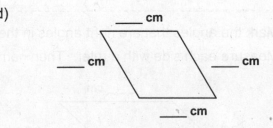

d) ____ cm   ____ cm   ____ cm   ____ cm

5. Complete the charts below. Use shapes **A** to **J** for each chart. Start by marking the right angles and parallel lines in each figure. If you are not sure if a figure is equilateral, measure its sides with a ruler.

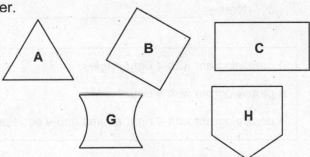

a)

Property	Shapes with Property
Equilateral	
Not Equilateral	

b)

Property	Shapes with Property
No right angle	
1 right angle	
2 right angles	
3 right angles	
4 right angles	

c)

Property	Shapes with Property
No obtuse angles	
1 or more obtuse angles	

d)

Property	Shapes with Property
No parallel sides	
1 pair of parallel sides	
2 pairs of parallel sides	
3 pairs of parallel sides	

e)

Polygon Name	Shapes with Property
Triangles	
Quadrilaterals	
Pentagons	
Hexagons	

NOTE: Polygons must have <u>straight</u> sides.

G6-12: Special Quadrilaterals

A **quadrilateral** (shape with 4 sides) with two pairs of parallel sides is called a **parallelogram**.

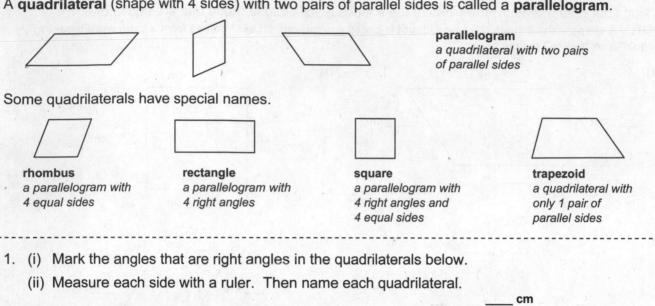

parallelogram
a quadrilateral with two pairs of parallel sides

Some quadrilaterals have special names.

rhombus
a parallelogram with 4 equal sides

rectangle
a parallelogram with 4 right angles

square
a parallelogram with 4 right angles and 4 equal sides

trapezoid
a quadrilateral with only 1 pair of parallel sides

----

1. (i) Mark the angles that are right angles in the quadrilaterals below.

   (ii) Measure each side with a ruler. Then name each quadrilateral.

   a)

   ____ cm

   ____ cm   ____ cm

   ____ cm

   Name: _____

   b)

   ____ cm

   ____ cm   ____ cm

   ____ cm

   Name: _____

2. Match the name of the quadrilateral to the best description.

Square	A parallelogram with 4 right angles.
Rectangle	A parallelogram with 4 equal sides.
Rhombus	A parallelogram with 4 right angles and 4 equal sides.

3. Name the shapes.
   HINT: Use the words rhombus, square, parallelogram and rectangle.

   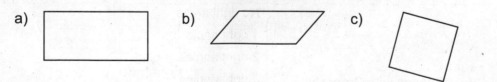

   a)   b)   c)   d)

   _____   _____   _____   _____

4. Mark all the right angles in each quadrilateral. Then identify each quadrilateral as a square, a rectangle, a parallelogram or a rhombus.

   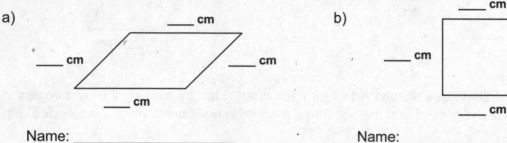

   a)   b)   c)   d)

   _____   _____   _____   _____

G6-12: Special Quadrilaterals (continued)

5. For each quadrilateral, say how many <u>pairs</u> of sides are parallel.
   Then identify each quadrilateral as a square, a rectangle, a parallelogram or a trapezoid.

   a)   b)   c)   d)

   _____ pairs   _____ pairs   _____   _____
   of parallel sides   of parallel sides

                                                           _____   _____

   _____   _____   _____   _____

6. The shape on the grid is a trapezoid.

   On the grid, draw a second trapezoid that has
   <u>no</u> right angles.

7. Use the words "all", "some", or "no" for each statement.

   a) _____ squares are rectangles   b) _____ trapezoids are parallelograms

   c) _____ parallelograms are trapezoids   d) _____ parallelograms are rectangles

8. a) I have 4 equal sides, but no right angles. What am I?

   b) I have 4 right angles, but my sides are not all equal. What am I? _____

   c) I have exactly 2 right angles. Which special quadrilateral could I be? _____

9. Write 3 different names for a square: _____ _____ _____

10. A shape has 4 right angles. Which two special quadrilaterals might it be?

11. On grid paper, draw a quadrilateral with …

    a) no right angles   b) one right angle   c) two right angles   d) no parallel sides

    e) one pair of parallel sides   f) two pairs of parallel sides and no right angles

12. Describe any similarities or differences between a …

    a) rhombus and a parallelogram   b) rhombus and a square   c) trapezoid and a parallelogram

13. a) Why is a square a rectangle?   b) Why is a rectangle not always a square?
    c) Why is a trapezoid not a parallelogram?

A **kite** is a quadrilateral with two pairs
of equal adjacent sides and no indentation.

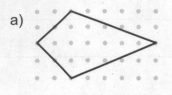

Adjacent sides are equal in length →

← *indentation*

<u>not</u> a kite

---

1. Measure the sides with a ruler. Which shapes are kites?

a)

b)

c)

d)

2. You can draw a diagonal by joining opposite vertices.
   Draw the diagonals of each shape in Question 1.

3. Measure the angles between the diagonals you drew in Question 1.
   What property do the kites have that the other shapes don't have?

4. a) Find the length of A, B, C and D.
      Which two lengths are the same?

   b) Predict a general rule for the diagonals of all kites.
      Draw 2 more kites on a grid or dot paper
      and test your prediction.

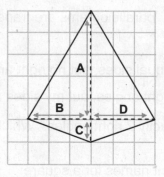

5. Measure the angles of the kites you drew. What do you notice?

6. Sort the shapes into the Venn diagram.

   A.   B. 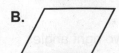   C.

   D.   E.   F.

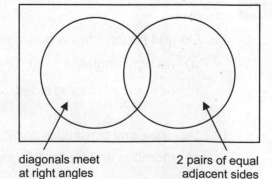

diagonals meet
at right angles

2 pairs of equal
adjacent sides

7. Find the name that fits best!

   a) A rhombus that is also a rectangle.   b) A parallelogram that is also a kite.

   c) A rectangle that is also a kite.   d) A kite that has equal opposite sides.

jump math
MULTIPLYING POTENTIAL.

Geometry 1

G6-14: Exploring Congruency

Shapes are **congruent** if they are **the same size** and **the same shape**. Congruent shapes can have different colours and patterns, and can be facing different directions.

These pairs of shapes are congruent:

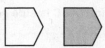  

---

1. Write <u>congruent</u> or <u>not congruent</u> under each pair of shapes.

   a) 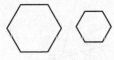   b) 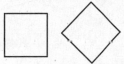   c)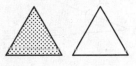

   <u>   not congruent   </u>   _____   _____

2. Are these pairs of shapes congruent?

   a)   _____ because _____

   b) 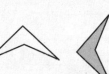 _____ because _____

3. a) Draw a parallelogram <u>congruent</u> to the one shown.

   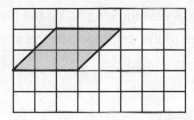

   b) Draw a trapezoid that is <u>not congruent</u> to the one shown.

   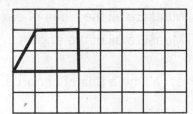

4. 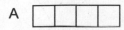 The picture shows one way to cut a 3 by 4 grid into 2 congruent shapes. Show how many ways you can cut a 3 by 4 grid into 2 congruent shapes.

5. a) On grid paper, show how many different (non-congruent) shapes you can make by adding one square to the original figure.

   A   B   C

   b) From which shape can you make the greatest number of non-congruent figures?

Geometry 1

Two triangles are **congruent** if:

a)   each **side** in one triangle has a corresponding side **of the same length** in the other triangle, and ...

b)   each **angle** in one triangle has a corresponding **angle of the same size** in the other triangle.

IMPORTANT: Sides are identified by their endpoints. For instance, the side marked by an 'X' in △ABC is side AB.

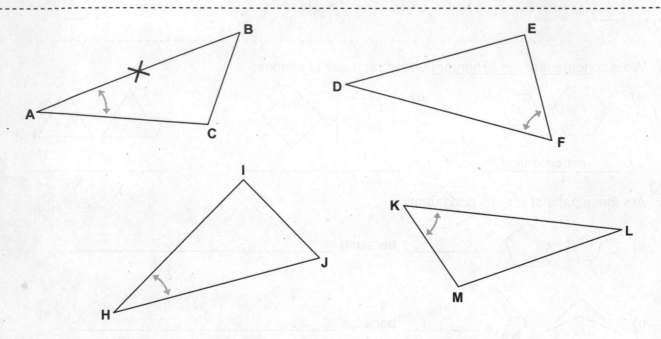

6.   Name the angle marked in each triangle:

a) in △ABC: __∠BAC__   b) in △DEF: _____   c) in △HIJ: _____   d) in △KLM: _____

7.   a)   Measure all the sides of each triangle to the nearest cm. Write the lengths on the triangles.

b)   Measure all of the angles in each triangle. Write the size of the angles inside the triangles.

8.   a)   Name a pair of congruent triangles.

b)   Name all pairs of equal sides for the triangles you picked.

c)   Name one pair of congruent angles from the triangles you picked.

9.   Measure the sides and angles of each figure below. Draw a figure that is congruent to the original.

a)

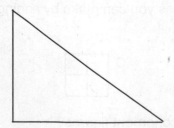

b)

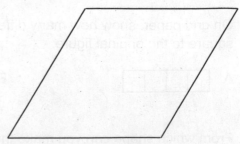

G6-15: Similarity

Two shapes are **similar** if they are the same <u>shape</u>. They **do not** need to be the same **size**.

Example:

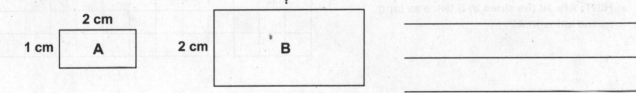

```
      3 cm
    ┌──────────┐                         6 cm
1 cm│    A     │              ┌───────────────────────┐
    └──────────┘         2 cm │          B            │
                              │                       │
                              └───────────────────────┘
```

Rectangles A and B are <u>similar</u>.

The width of B (2 cm) is two times the width of A (1 cm). Since A and B are the same shape, the length of B must also be two times the length of A – and it is (6 cm vs. 3 cm).

----

1. Rectangles A and B are similar. How can you find the length of B without a ruler?

```
        2 cm                        ?
     ┌────────┐           ┌──────────────────┐
1 cm │   A    │      2 cm │        B         │
     └────────┘           │                  │
                          └──────────────────┘
```
    _____

    _____

    _____

2. Rectangles A and B are similar. How many times the width of A is the width of B?

    a) width of A: 1 cm   width of B: 3 cm   b) width of A: 2 cm   width of B: 6 cm

    The width of B is _____ times the width of A.   The width of B is _____ times the width of A.

    c) width of A: 2 cm   width of B: 10 cm   d) width of A: 3 cm   width of B: 12 cm

    The width of B is _____ times the width of A.   The width of B is _____ times the width of A.

3. Rectangles A and B are similar. Find the length of B.

    a) width of A: 1 cm   width of B: 2 cm   b) width of A: 1 cm   width of B: 3 cm

    length of A: 3 cm   length of B: _____   length of A: 5 cm   length of B: _____

    c) width of A: 2 cm   width of B: 6 cm   d) width of A: 5 cm   width of B: 10 cm

    length of A: 4 cm   length of B: _____   length of A: 10 cm   length of B: _____

4. Rectangle A and rectangle B are similar. On grid paper, draw rectangle A. Then draw B.

    a) width of A: 1 unit   b) width of A: 1 unit   c) width of A: 2 units

    length of A: 2 units   length of A: 2 units   length of A: 3 units

    width of B: 2 units   width of B: 3 units   width of B: 4 units

    length of B: ?   length of B: ?   length of B: ?

G6-15: Similarity (continued)

5. Draw a trapezoid similar to A, with a base that is two times as long as the base of A.
   HINT: A is 1 unit high. How high should the new figure be?

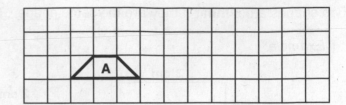

6.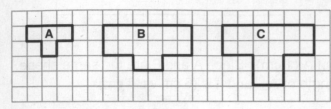

   Which of these shapes are similar? How do you know?

7. Are shapes A and B similar?
   Explain how you know.
   HINT: Are all the sides in B twice as long as the sides in A?

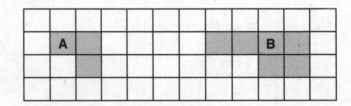

8. Triangle A and Triangle B are the same height.
   Which triangle is similar to A:
   B or C?
   How do you know?

9. Which shapes are congruent? Which are similar?

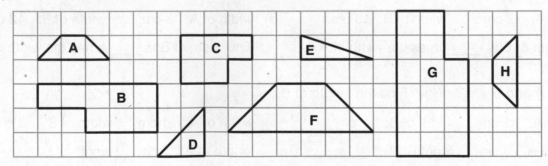

10. Draw a parallelogram on grid paper.
    Then, draw a similar parallelogram that is exactly twice as high as the first.

11. Draw a right-angled triangle on grid paper.
    Then, draw a similar triangle that is exactly three times as high as the first.

12. If the corresponding angles in two triangles are all the same, the triangles are similar.
    Use a protractor and a ruler to construct two triangles that are similar but not congruent.

13. Can a trapezoid and a square ever be similar? Explain.

 jump math
MULTIPLYING POTENTIAL

Geometry 1

G6-16: Symmetry

Some shapes have lines of **symmetry**. Tina uses a mirror to check for symmetry in shapes. She places the mirror across half the shape and checks to see if the half reflected in the mirror makes her picture 'whole' again.

 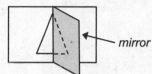 *mirror*

> **NOTE:**
> The two sides on either side of the mirror line are congruent.

Tina also checks if a shape has a line of symmetry by cutting the shape out and then folding it. If the halves of the shapes on either side of the fold match exactly, Tina knows that the fold shows a line of symmetry.

---

1. Complete the picture so that the dotted line is a line of symmetry.

a) 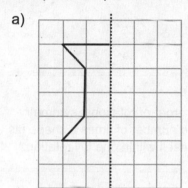   b) 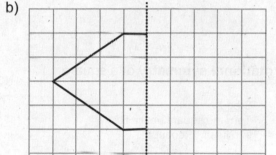   c)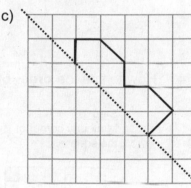

d) 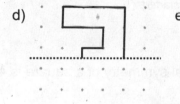   e) 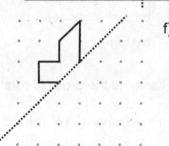   f) 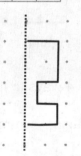   g)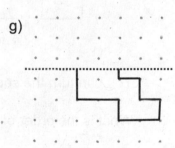

2. The shapes on either side of the mirror line below are <u>almost</u> congruent. Add one square so that the two are congruent. Then mark P on the other side of the mirror line.

a) 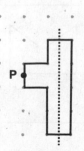   b) 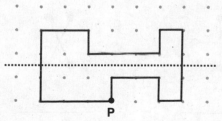   c)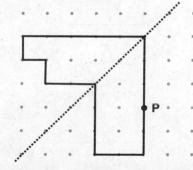

 jump math
MULTIPLYING POTENTIAL

Geometry 1

3. The dotted lines are lines of symmetry for a figure. Draw the missing parts of the figure.
   HINT: Use the lines as mirror lines.

a)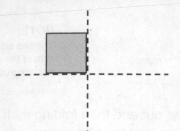

b)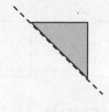

c)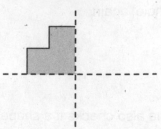

d)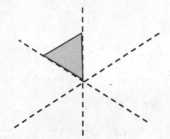

e)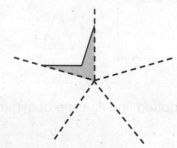

f)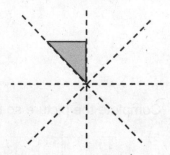

4. How to find the **order of rotational symmetry** of a square:

Step 1:
Mark any corner of the square.

Step 2:
Turn the square until it fits into itself. Repeat.

NOTE:
The order of rotational symmetry is the number of times a shape fits into itself within one full rotation.

$\frac{1}{4}$ turn $\frac{1}{2}$ turn $\frac{3}{4}$ turn   full turn

← *We stop now, since the marked corner is back where it started.*

You can turn the square 4 ways to fit into itself, so the order of rotational symmetry of a square is **4**.

What is the order of rotational symmetry of the following figures?

a)

b)

c)

d)

e)

f)

g)

h)

G6-16: Symmetry (continued)

5. Shade two shapes with exactly one line of symmetry.

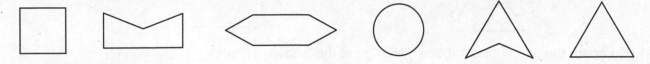

6. a) Sort the shapes according to the number of lines of symmetry they have.

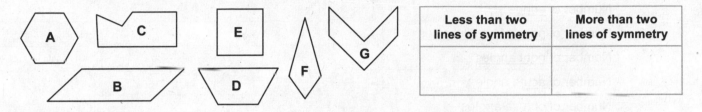

Less than two lines of symmetry	More than two lines of symmetry

b) Which two figures above have no lines of symmetry? _____ and _____

7. Draw all the lines of symmetry for each regular shape below. Then complete the chart provided.
   NOTE: "Regular" means having all angles and sides equal.

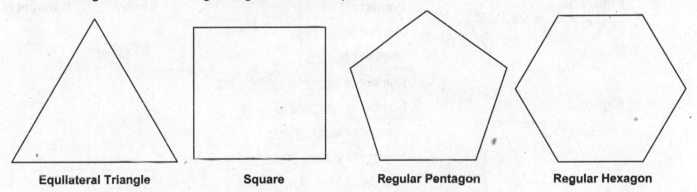

Equilateral Triangle　　　Square　　　Regular Pentagon　　　Regular Hexagon

a)

Figure	Triangle	Square	Pentagon	Hexagon
Number of edges				
Number of lines of symmetry				

b) Describe any relation you see between lines of symmetry and the number of edges.

c) Find the order of rotational symmetry for each shape.
   Describe any patterns you see.

8. Brenda says the line shown is a line of symmetry:
   Is she correct? Explain.

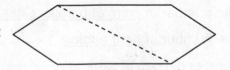

9. On grid paper, draw a figure with <u>exactly</u> two lines of symmetry.
   Explain how you know there are exactly two lines of symmetry.

 jump math
MULTIPLYING POTENTIAL

Geometry 1

G6-17: Comparing Shapes

1. **Figure 1:**   **Figure 2:**

a) Compare the two shapes above by filling out the following chart.

Property	Figure 1	Figure 2	Same?	Different?
Number of <u>vertices</u>	3	4		✓
Number of <u>edges</u>				
Number of <u>pairs of parallel sides</u>				
Number of <u>right angles</u>				
Number of <u>acute angles</u>				
Number of <u>obtuse angles</u>				
Number of <u>lines of symmetry</u>				
Is the figure <u>equilateral</u>?				

b) By simply looking at the following figures, can you say how they are the same and different?

Figure 1:

Figure 2:

Property	Same?	Different?
Number of <u>vertices</u>		
Number of <u>edges</u>		
Number of <u>pairs of parallel sides</u>		
Number of <u>right angles</u>		
Number of <u>acute angles</u>		
Number of <u>obtuse angles</u>		
Number of <u>lines of symmetry</u>		
Is the figure <u>equilateral</u>?		

2. Draw two figures and compare them using a chart (as in Question 1).

3. Looking at the following figures, can you comment on their **similarities** and **differences**?
    Be sure to mention the following properties:

    ✓ The number of <u>vertices</u>
    ✓ The number of <u>edges</u>
    ✓ The number of <u>pairs of parallel sides</u>   **Figure 1:** 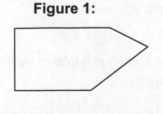   **Figure 2:**
    ✓ The number of <u>right angles</u>
    ✓ Number of <u>lines of symmetry</u>
    ✓ Whether the figure is <u>equilateral</u>
    ✓ Whether the figure has <u>rotational symmetry</u>

1. The following figures can be sorted by their properties:

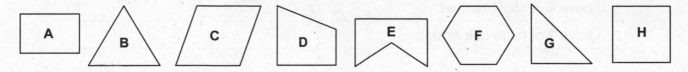

a)

Property	Figures with this property:
1. I am a quadrilateral	A, C, D, H
2. I am equilateral	B, C, F, H

Which figures share both properties? _____

Using the information in the chart above, complete the following Venn diagram.
NOTE: If a shape does not have either property, write its letter inside the box, but outside both circles.

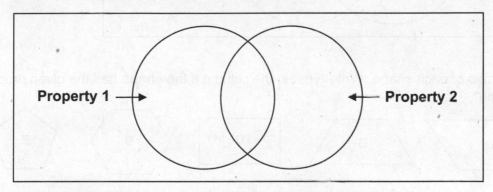

Using figures A through H above, complete the Venn diagrams below.

b)

Property	Figures with this property:
1. I am equilateral	
2. I have <u>no</u> right angles	

Which figures share both properties? _____

Using the information in the chart above, complete the following Venn diagram.

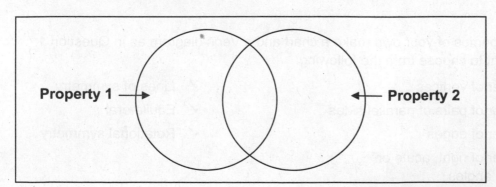

c)

Property	Figures with this property:
1. I have 4 or more vertices	
2. I have 2 or more obtuse angles	

Which figures share both properties? _____

Using the information in the chart above, complete the following Venn diagram.

Property 1 →   ← Property 2

2. Record the properties of each shape. Write "yes" in the column if the shape has the given property. Otherwise, write "no".

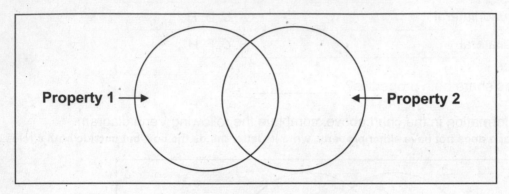

A   B   C   D   E

Shape	Quadrilateral	Equilateral	Two or more pairs of parallel sides	At least one right angle	At least one acute angle	At least one obtuse angle
A						
B						
C						
D						
E						

3. Using two properties of your own make a chart and a Venn diagram as in Question 1.
    You might want to choose from the following:

    ✓ Number of vertices
    ✓ Number of pairs of parallel sides
    ✓ Number of edges
    ✓ Number of right, acute or obtuse angles

    ✓ Lines of symmetry
    ✓ Equilateral
    ✓ Rotational symmetry

G6-19: Sorting & Classifying Shapes (Advanced)

1. Write **T** (for true) if <u>both</u> figures have the property in common. Otherwise, write **F** (for false).

   Both figures have ...

   a)

   _____ 4 vertices   _____ 2 pairs of parallel sides

   _____ 4 sides   _____ 2 right angles

   b)

   _____ 3 vertices   _____ 5 sides

   _____ no right angles _____ equilateral

   c)

   _____ 3 sides   _____ 1 pair of parallel sides

   _____ 1 obtuse angle _____ at least 1 acute angle

   d)

   _____ 4 sides   _____ 1 pair of parallel sides

   _____ 2 right angles _____ 4 vertices

   e)

   _____ quadrilateral   _____ at least 1 right angle

   _____ at least 1 pair of parallel sides

   _____ 2 pairs of parallel sides

   f)

   _____ 6 vertices

   _____ at least 2 pairs of parallel sides

   _____ no right angles   _____ equilateral

2. a) I have three sides. All of my sides are the same length. I'm an ...

   _____

   b) I have three sides. Two of my sides are the same length. I'm an ...

   _____

   c) I am a quadrilateral with two pairs of parallel sides. I'm a ...

   _____

   d) I am a quadrilateral with exactly one pair of parallel sides. I'm a ...

   _____

3. Describe each figure completely.

   In your description you should mention the properties listed in Question 3 in the previous section.

   a)

   b)
   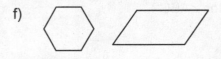

   c)

4. Name all the properties the figures have in common. Then describe any differences.

   a)
   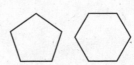

   b)

Geometry 1

G6-20: Puzzles and Problems

Answer the questions below in your notebook.

1. Copy the following figures onto cm grid paper.

   Be sure to be exact.

   i) Measure the sides and angles of each figure.

   ii) Name each figure. (Explain how you know what kind of figure you drew.)

   a)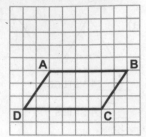
   b)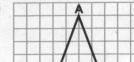

2. Using a ruler and a protractor, construct: a) a parallelogram b) a rhombus c) an isosceles triangle

3. a) Estimate the size of ∠ABC and ∠DEF. Which angle is greater?

   b) How can you use the grid to give an exact measurement for ∠ABC?

   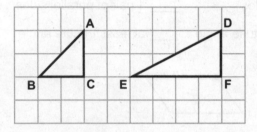

4. Copy the shape onto grid paper and mark:
   • 2 acute angles with a single line,
   • 2 obtuse angles with a double line, and
   • 4 right angles with a square.

   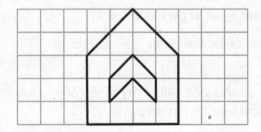

5. Which of the quadrilaterals have only one name? Which have two? Which have three?
   Write as many names as you can for each figure.

   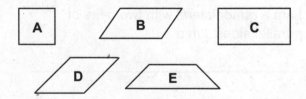

6. Circle the acute angles in each triangle. One of the triangles has a right angle. Can you find it?

   a)   b)   c)

7. Name the triangles:
   a) I have three equal sides.
   b) I have one angle greater than a right angle.
   c) I have one right angle.
   d) I have 3 angles less than 90°.

jump math
MULTIPLYING POTENTIAL.

Geometry 1